Orthorexia Nervosa Workbook

Daily / Weekly Practical Worksheets Inspired by Behavioral and Exposure Therapy to Help Treat Orthorexia

Copyritght 2021 © Mesloub Iheb

All Rights Reserved.

For My Self-esteem, I Swear :

ORTHOREXIA
Daily Symptoms Checklist

	SEVERITY	MON	TUES	WED	THUR	FRI	SAT	SUN
WORRYING ABOUT FOOD QUALITY	0-10 Y/N							
AVOID DINING OUT OR CONSUMING FOOD THAT HAS BEEN PREPARED BY OTHERS.	0-10 Y/N							
I'M AFRAID OF BECOMING ILL.	0-10 Y/N							
MANIFEST BODILY INDICATIONS OF MALNUTRITION	0-10 Y/N							
INVEST YOUR TIME ON FOOD RESEARCH.	0-10 Y/N							
REFUSING TO CONSUME A WIDE VARIETY OF MEALS	0-10 Y/N							
YOU'RE AFRAID OF LOSING CONTROL.	0-10 Y/N							
DON'T BE TOO HARSH ON YOUR FRIENDS' EATING CHOICES.	Y/N 0-10							
YOU'RE AFRAID OF LOSING CONTROL.	0-10 Y/N							

ORTHOREXIA
DBT RECOVERY WORKSHEET

Date: / /

Sleep quality:

IDENTIFY STRESS-INDUCING BEHAVIORS (ORTHOREXIC BEHAVIORS) AND BELIEFS, THEN REPLACE THEM WITH MORE FLEXIBLE THOUGHTS AND ACTIONS.

Daily Mood Checker ✓

- [ ] ANGRY
- [ ] ANNOYED
- [ ] ANXIOUS
- [ ] ASHAMED
- [ ] AWKWARD
- [ ] BRAVE
- [ ] CALM
- [ ] CHEERFUL
- [ ] CHILL
- [ ] CONFUSED
- [ ] DISCOURAGED
- [ ] DISTRACTED
- [ ] EMBARRASSED
- [ ] EXCITED
- [ ] FRIENDLY
- [ ] GUILTY
- [ ] HAPPY
- [ ] HOPEFUL
- [ ] LONELY
- [ ] LOVED
- [ ] NERVOUS
- [ ] OFFENDED
- [ ] SCARED
- [ ] THOUGHTFUL
- [ ] TIRED
- [ ] UNCOMFORTABLE
- [ ] UNSURE

✓ __:__

✓ __:__

✓ __:__

A DAILY WIN

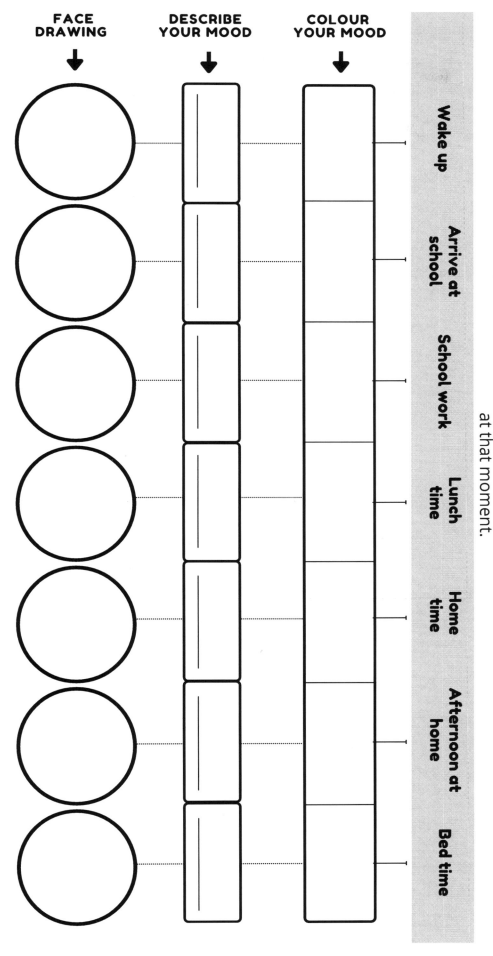

OVERCOMING ORTHOREXIA EPISODES

> In this schedule, try to remain conscious of the nature of this disorder
> Discuss its effect on your feelings and actions, what coping skills do you think work when used at the right time, and how well have you applied these skills?

Orthorexic Behaviors	Awareness About Orthorexic Behaviors: Coping skills used or Prevention methods
	👍 : ✋ :

DATE :   /   /

RATE YOUR PSYCHOLOGICAL SATISFACTION : .... /10

WEEKLY EXPOSURE THERAPY WORKSHEET TO GET RIDE OF ORTHOREXIA

This worksheet is useful for eliminating orthorexic behaviors for those with Orthorexia

Exposure therapy depends on confronting the causes of the problem with courage. So, try to go to a restaurant that serves healthy foods. Take an unhealthy food with you, such as burger slices with pizza, and put it with the food served to you. You will have specific obsessions. Try to overcome these obsessions and eat all your food. *The goal of this procedure is to break the obsession by being bravely exposed to it, and by doing so you will get used to it.*	**TASK** ☐ OBSESSION ○ ○ ○ ○ ○
Organize or take part in a tour with your friends towards a respectable restaurant. Try to confront your fears about the food served to you. Try to enjoy your time with them at the same time. Do not think about the quality of the food too much, because fear leads to anxiety. *This exercise will stimulate your subconscious mind to eliminate the fear of poor quality food, and maintain your social relationships*	**TASK** ☐ ANXIETY / FEAR OF FOOD ○ ○ ○ ○ ○
Go to a nearby mountain. Try to camp or sit in it for hours. There, do activities you like, such as reading a book, meditation exercises, yoga, a specific sport. *Take a variety of food.* .... *Reducing anxiety is a major goal of getting rid of this disorder and this procedure will help you build a balance in your feelings*	**TASK** ☐ ENJOYMENT ○ ○ ○ ○ ○

ONE WAY TO MAKE TOMORROW BETTER:

....

....

ORTHOREXIA
Daily Symptoms Checklist

	SEVERITY	MON	TUES	WED	THUR	FRI	SAT	SUN
WORRYING ABOUT FOOD QUALITY	0-10 Y/N							
AVOID DINING OUT OR CONSUMING FOOD THAT HAS BEEN PREPARED BY OTHERS.	0-10 Y/N							
I'M AFRAID OF BECOMING ILL.	0-10 Y/N							
MANIFEST BODILY INDICATIONS OF MALNUTRITION	0-10 Y/N							
INVEST YOUR TIME ON FOOD RESEARCH.	0-10 Y/N							
REFUSING TO CONSUME A WIDE VARIETY OF MEALS	0-10 Y/N							
YOU'RE AFRAID OF LOSING CONTROL.	0-10 Y/N							
DON'T BE TOO HARSH ON YOUR FRIENDS' EATING CHOICES.	Y/N 0-10							
YOU'RE AFRAID OF LOSING CONTROL.	0-10 Y/N							

ORTHOREXIA
DBT RECOVERY WORKSHEET

Date: / /

Sleep quality:

IDENTIFY STRESS-INDUCING BEHAVIORS (ORTHOREXIC BEHAVIORS) AND BELIEFS, THEN REPLACE THEM WITH MORE FLEXIBLE THOUGHTS AND ACTIONS.

Daily Mood Checker

- ANGRY ☐
- ANNOYED ☐
- ANXIOUS ☐
- ASHAMED ☐
- AWKWARD ☐
- BRAVE ☐
- CALM ☐
- CHEERFUL ☐
- CHILL ☐
- CONFUSED ☐
- DISCOURAGED ☐
- DISTRACTED ☐
- EMBARRASSED ☐
- EXCITED ☐
- FRIENDLY ☐
- GUILTY ☐
- HAPPY ☐
- HOPEFUL ☐
- LONELY ☐
- LOVED ☐
- NERVOUS ☐
- OFFENDED ☐
- SCARED ☐
- THOUGHTFUL ☐
- TIRED ☐
- UNCOMFORTABLE ☐
- UNSURE ☐

✓ __:__

✓ __:__

✓ __:__

A DAILY WIN

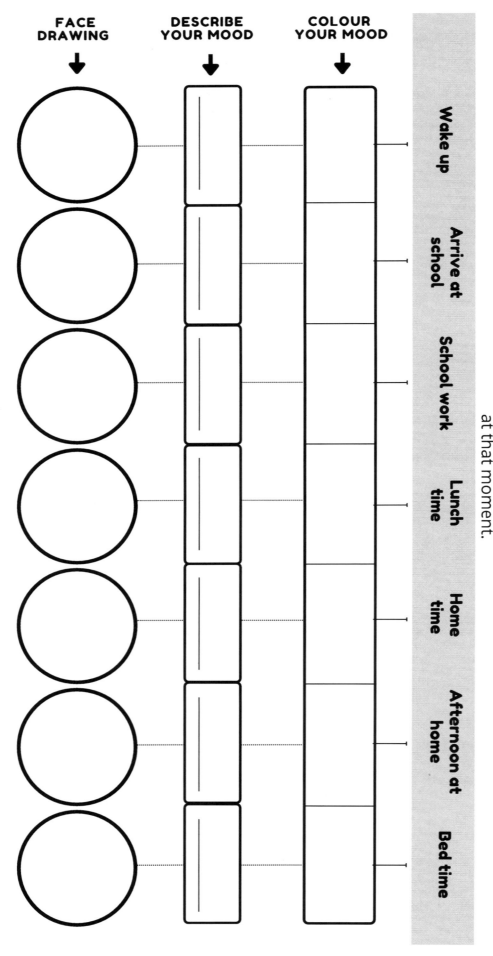

OVERCOMING ORTHOREXIA EPISODES

In this schedule, try to remain conscious of the nature of this disorder
Discuss its effect on your feelings and actions, what coping skills do you think work when used at the right time, and how well have you applied these skills?

Orthorexic Behaviors	Awareness About Orthorexic Behaviors: Coping skills used or Prevention methods
	👍 : ✋ :

DATE : __ / __ / __

RATE YOUR PSYCHOLOGICAL SATISFACTION : …. / 10

WEEKLY EXPOSURE THERAPY WORKSHEET TO GET RIDE OF ORTHOREXIA

This worksheet is useful for eliminating orthorexic behaviors for those with Orthorexia

Exposure therapy depends on confronting the causes of the problem with courage. So, try to go to a restaurant that serves healthy foods. Take an unhealthy food with you, such as burger slices with pizza, and put it with the food served to you. You will have specific obsessions. Try to overcome these obsessions and eat all your food. *The goal of this procedure is to break the obsession by being bravely exposed to it, and by doing so you will get used to it.*	**TASK** ☐ OBSESSION ○ ○ ○ ○ ○
Organize or take part in a tour with your friends towards a respectable restaurant. Try to confront your fears about the food served to you. Try to enjoy your time with them at the same time. Do not think about the quality of the food too much, because fear leads to anxiety. *This exercise will stimulate your subconscious mind to eliminate the fear of poor quality food, and maintain your social relationships*	**TASK** ☐ ANXIETY / FEAR OF FOOD ○ ○ ○ ○ ○
Go to a nearby mountain. Try to camp or sit in it for hours. There, do activities you like, such as reading a book, meditation exercises, yoga, a specific sport. Take a variety of food. ………….. *Reducing anxiety is a major goal of getting rid of this disorder and this procedure will help you build a balance in your feelings*	**TASK** ☐ ENJOYMENT ○ ○ ○ ○ ○

ONE WAY TO MAKE TOMORROW BETTER:

………………………………………………………………………………………………

………………………………………………………………………………………………

ORTHOREXIA
DBT RECOVERY WORKSHEET

Date: / /

Sleep quality:

IDENTIFY STRESS-INDUCING BEHAVIORS (ORTHOREXIC BEHAVIORS) AND BELIEFS, THEN REPLACE THEM WITH MORE FLEXIBLE THOUGHTS AND ACTIONS.

Daily Mood Checker

- [ ] ANGRY
- [ ] ANNOYED
- [ ] ANXIOUS
- [ ] ASHAMED
- [ ] AWKWARD
- [ ] BRAVE
- [ ] CALM
- [ ] CHEERFUL
- [ ] CHILL
- [ ] CONFUSED
- [ ] DISCOURAGED
- [ ] DISTRACTED
- [ ] EMBARRASSED
- [ ] EXCITED
- [ ] FRIENDLY
- [ ] GUILTY
- [ ] HAPPY
- [ ] HOPEFUL
- [ ] LONELY
- [ ] LOVED
- [ ] NERVOUS
- [ ] OFFENDED
- [ ] SCARED
- [ ] THOUGHTFUL
- [ ] TIRED
- [ ] UNCOMFORTABLE
- [ ] UNSURE

A DAILY WIN

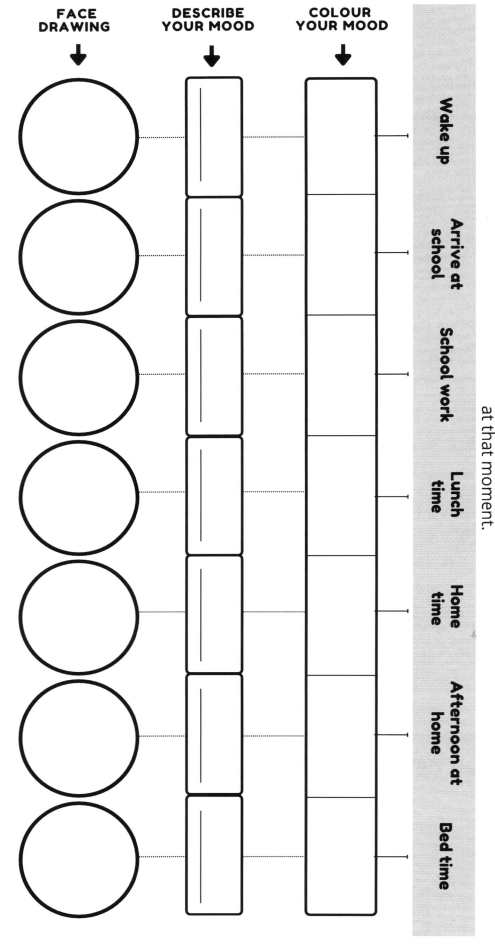

OVERCOMING ORTHOREXIA EPISODES

> In this schedule, try to remain conscious of the nature of this disorder
> Discuss its effect on your feelings and actions, what coping skills do you think work when used at the right time, and how well have you applied these skills?

Orthorexic Behaviors	Awareness About Orthorexic Behaviors: Coping skills used or Prevention methods
	👍 : ✋ :

ORTHOREXIA
Daily Symptoms Checklist

	SEVERITY	MON	TUES	WED	THUR	FRI	SAT	SUN
WORRYING ABOUT FOOD QUALITY	0-10 Y/N							
AVOID DINING OUT OR CONSUMING FOOD THAT HAS BEEN PREPARED BY OTHERS.	0-10 Y/N							
I'M AFRAID OF BECOMING ILL.	0-10 Y/N							
MANIFEST BODILY INDICATIONS OF MALNUTRITION	0-10 Y/N							
INVEST YOUR TIME ON FOOD RESEARCH.	0-10 Y/N							
REFUSING TO CONSUME A WIDE VARIETY OF MEALS	0-10 Y/N							
YOU'RE AFRAID OF LOSING CONTROL.	0-10 Y/N							
DON'T BE TOO HARSH ON YOUR FRIENDS' EATING CHOICES.	Y/N 0-10							
YOU'RE AFRAID OF LOSING CONTROL.	0-10 Y/N							

ORTHOREXIA
DBT RECOVERY WORKSHEET

Date: / /

Sleep quality:

IDENTIFY STRESS-INDUCING BEHAVIORS (ORTHOREXIC BEHAVIORS) AND BELIEFS, THEN REPLACE THEM WITH MORE FLEXIBLE THOUGHTS AND ACTIONS.

Daily Mood Checker

✓ ___ : ___

_____
_____
_____

✓ ___ : ___

_____
_____
_____

✓ ___ : ___

_____
_____
_____

- ANGRY ☐
- ANNOYED ☐
- ANXIOUS ☐
- ASHAMED ☐
- AWKWARD ☐
- BRAVE ☐
- CALM ☐
- CHEERFUL ☐
- CHILL ☐
- CONFUSED ☐
- DISCOURAGED ☐
- DISTRACTED ☐
- EMBARRASSED ☐
- EXCITED ☐
- FRIENDLY ☐
- GUILTY ☐
- HAPPY ☐
- HOPEFUL ☐
- LONELY ☐
- LOVED ☐
- NERVOUS ☐
- OFFENDED ☐
- SCARED ☐
- THOUGHTFUL ☐
- TIRED ☐
- UNCOMFORTABLE ☐
- UNSURE ☐

A DAILY WIN

_____
_____
_____

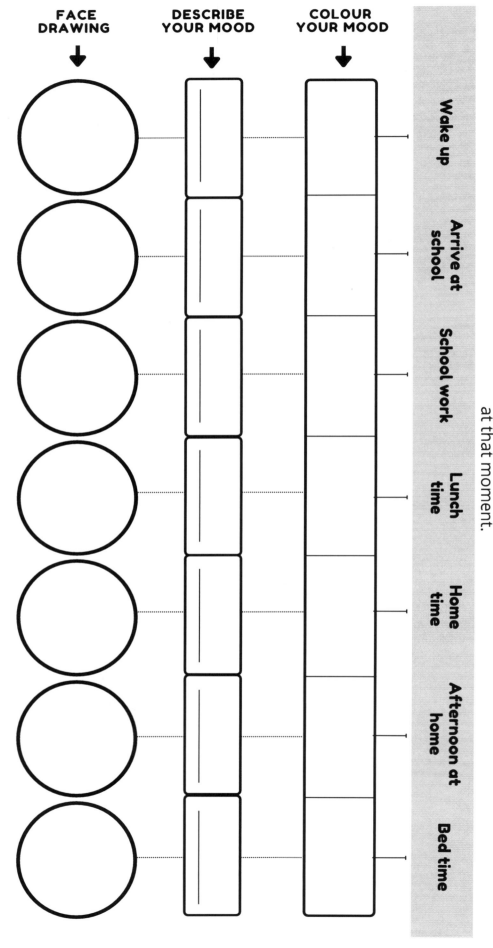

OVERCOMING ORTHOREXIA EPISODES

In this schedule, try to remain conscious of the nature of this disorder
Discuss its effect on your feelings and actions, what coping skills do you think work when used at the right time, and how well have you applied these skills?

Orthorexic Behaviors	Awareness About Orthorexic Behaviors: Coping skills used or Prevention methods
	👍 : ✋ :

DATE :   /   /

RATE YOUR PSYCHOLOGICAL SATISFACTION : .... /10

WEEKLY EXPOSURE THERAPY WORKSHEET TO GET RIDE OF ORTHOREXIA

This worksheet is useful for eliminating orthorexic behaviors for those with Orthorexia

Description	Task
Exposure therapy depends on confronting the causes of the problem with courage. So, try to go to a restaurant that serves healthy foods. Take an unhealthy food with you, such as burger slices with pizza, and put it with the food served to you. You will have specific obsessions. Try to overcome these obsessions and eat all your food. *The goal of this procedure is to break the obsession by being bravely exposed to it, and by doing so you will get used to it.*	**TASK** ☐ OBSESSION ○ ○ ○ ○ ○
Organize or take part in a tour with your friends towards a respectable restaurant. Try to confront your fears about the food served to you. Try to enjoy your time with them at the same time. Do not think about the quality of the food too much, because fear leads to anxiety. *This exercise will stimulate your subconscious mind to eliminate the fear of poor quality food, and maintain your social relationships*	**TASK** ☐ ANXIETY / FEAR OF FOOD ○ ○ ○ ○ ○
Go to a nearby mountain. Try to camp or sit in it for hours. There, do activities you like, such as reading a book, meditation exercises, yoga, a specific sport. Take a variety of food. .... *Reducing anxiety is a major goal of getting rid of this disorder and this procedure will help you build a balance in your feelings*	**TASK** ☐ ENJOYMENT ○ ○ ○ ○ ○

ONE WAY TO MAKE TOMORROW BETTER:

....

....

ORTHOREXIA
DBT RECOVERY WORKSHEET

Date: / /

Sleep quality:

IDENTIFY STRESS-INDUCING BEHAVIORS (ORTHOREXIC BEHAVIORS) AND BELIEFS, THEN REPLACE THEM WITH MORE FLEXIBLE THOUGHTS AND ACTIONS.

✓ ___ : ___

_____
_____
_____

✓ ___ : ___

_____
_____
_____

✓ ___ : ___

_____
_____
_____

A DAILY WIN

_____
_____
_____

Daily Mood Checker

- ANGRY ☐
- ANNOYED ☐
- ANXIOUS ☐
- ASHAMED ☐
- AWKWARD ☐
- BRAVE ☐
- CALM ☐
- CHEERFUL ☐
- CHILL ☐
- CONFUSED ☐
- DISCOURAGED ☐
- DISTRACTED ☐
- EMBARRASSED ☐
- EXCITED ☐
- FRIENDLY ☐
- GUILTY ☐
- HAPPY ☐
- HOPEFUL ☐
- LONELY ☐
- LOVED ☐
- NERVOUS ☐
- OFFENDED ☐
- SCARED ☐
- THOUGHTFUL ☐
- TIRED ☐
- UNCOMFORTABLE ☐
- UNSURE ☐

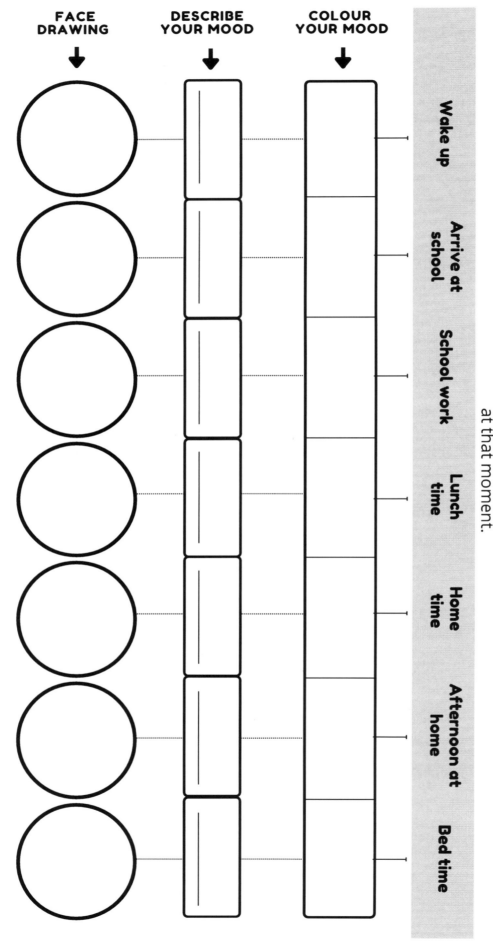

OVERCOMING ORTHOREXIA EPISODES

> In this schedule, try to remain conscious of the nature of this disorder
> Discuss its effect on your feelings and actions, what coping skills do you think work when used at the right time, and how well have you applied these skills?

Orthorexic Behaviors	Awareness About Orthorexic Behaviors: Coping skills used or Prevention methods
	👍 : ✋ :

ORTHORAXIA
Daily Symptoms Checklist

	SEVERITY	MON	TUES	WED	THUR	FRI	SAT	SUN
WORRYING ABOUT FOOD QUALITY	0-10 Y/N							
AVOID DINING OUT OR CONSUMING FOOD THAT HAS BEEN PREPARED BY OTHERS.	0-10 Y/N							
I'M AFRAID OF BECOMING ILL.	0-10 Y/N							
MANIFEST BODILY INDICATIONS OF MALNUTRITION	0-10 Y/N							
INVEST YOUR TIME ON FOOD RESEARCH.	0-10 Y/N							
REFUSING TO CONSUME A WIDE VARIETY OF MEALS	0-10 Y/N							
YOU'RE AFRAID OF LOSING CONTROL.	0-10 Y/N							
DON'T BE TOO HARSH ON YOUR FRIENDS' EATING CHOICES.	Y/N 0-10							
YOU'RE AFRAID OF LOSING CONTROL.	0-10 Y/N							

ORTHOREXIA
DBT RECOVERY WORKSHEET

Date: / /
Sleep quality:

IDENTIFY STRESS-INDUCING BEHAVIORS (ORTHOREXIC BEHAVIORS) AND BELIEFS, THEN REPLACE THEM WITH MORE FLEXIBLE THOUGHTS AND ACTIONS.

Daily Mood Checker

✓ ___:___

- ANGRY ☐
- ANNOYED ☐
- ANXIOUS ☐
- ASHAMED ☐
- AWKWARD ☐
- BRAVE ☐
- CALM ☐
- CHEERFUL ☐
- CHILL ☐
- CONFUSED ☐

✓ ___:___

- DISCOURAGED ☐
- DISTRACTED ☐
- EMBARRASSED ☐
- EXCITED ☐
- FRIENDLY ☐
- GUILTY ☐

✓ ___:___

- HAPPY ☐
- HOPEFUL ☐
- LONELY ☐
- LOVED ☐
- NERVOUS ☐
- OFFENDED ☐
- SCARED ☐
- THOUGHTFUL ☐
- TIRED ☐
- UNCOMFORTABLE ☐
- UNSURE ☐

A DAILY WIN

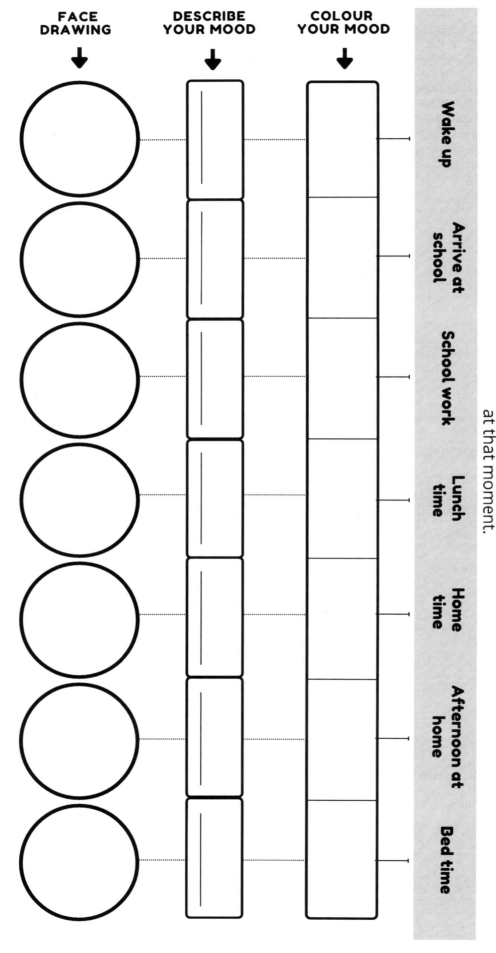

OVERCOMING ORTHOREXIA EPISODES

> In this schedule, try to remain conscious of the nature of this disorder
> Discuss its effect on your feelings and actions, what coping skills do you think work when used at the right time, and how well have you applied these skills?

Orthorexic Behaviors	Awareness About Orthorexic Behaviors: Coping skills used or Prevention methods
	👍 : ✋ :

DATE : / /

RATE YOUR PSYCHOLOGICAL SATISFACTION : .... /10

WEEKLY EXPOSURE THERAPY WORKSHEET TO GET RIDE OF ORTHOREXIA

This worksheet is useful for eliminating orthorexic behaviors for those with Orthorexia

Exposure therapy depends on confronting the causes of the problem with courage. So, try to go to a restaurant that serves healthy foods. Take an unhealthy food with you, such as burger slices with pizza, and put it with the food served to you. You will have specific obsessions. Try to overcome these obsessions and eat all your food. *The goal of this procedure is to break the obsession by being bravely exposed to it, and by doing so you will get used to it.*	**TASK** ☐ OBSESSION ○○○○○
Organize or take part in a tour with your friends towards a respectable restaurant. Try to confront your fears about the food served to you. Try to enjoy your time with them at the same time. Do not think about the quality of the food too much, because fear leads to anxiety. *This exercise will stimulate your subconscious mind to eliminate the fear of poor quality food, and maintain your social relationships*	**TASK** ☐ ANXIETY / FEAR OF FOOD ○○○○○
Go to a nearby mountain. Try to camp or sit in it for hours. There, do activities you like, such as reading a book, meditation exercises, yoga, a specific sport. *Take a variety of food.* .... *Reducing anxiety is a major goal of getting rid of this disorder and this procedure will help you build a balance in your feelings*	**TASK** ☐ ENJOYMENT ○○○○○

ONE WAY TO MAKE TOMORROW BETTER:

....

....

ORTHOREXIA
DBT RECOVERY WORKSHEET

Date: / /

Sleep quality:

IDENTIFY STRESS-INDUCING BEHAVIORS (ORTHOREXIC BEHAVIORS) AND BELIEFS, THEN REPLACE THEM WITH MORE FLEXIBLE THOUGHTS AND ACTIONS.

✓ ___ : ___

_____
_____
_____
_____

✓ ___ : ___

_____
_____
_____
_____

✓ ___ : ___

_____
_____
_____
_____

A DAILY WIN

_____
_____
_____

Daily Mood Checker ✓

- ANGRY ☐
- ANNOYED ☐
- ANXIOUS ☐
- ASHAMED ☐
- AWKWARD ☐
- BRAVE ☐
- CALM ☐
- CHEERFUL ☐
- CHILL ☐
- CONFUSED ☐
- DISCOURAGED ☐
- DISTRACTED ☐
- EMBARRASSED ☐
- EXCITED ☐
- FRIENDLY ☐
- GUILTY ☐
- HAPPY ☐
- HOPEFUL ☐
- LONELY ☐
- LOVED ☐
- NERVOUS ☐
- OFFENDED ☐
- SCARED ☐
- THOUGHTFUL ☐
- TIRED ☐
- UNCOMFORTABLE ☐
- UNSURE ☐

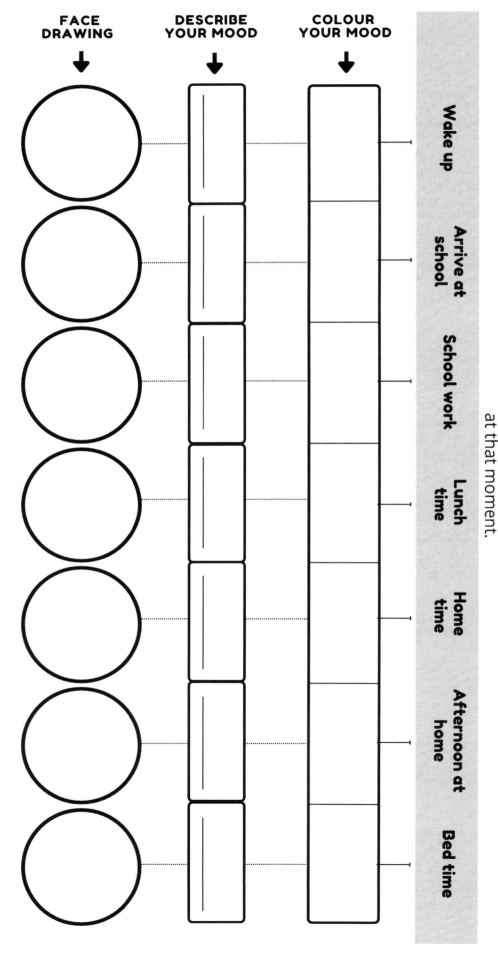

OVERCOMING ORTHOREXIA EPISODES

> In this schedule, try to remain conscious of the nature of this disorder
> Discuss its effect on your feelings and actions, what coping skills do you think work when used at the right time, and how well have you applied these skills?

Orthorexic Behaviors	Awareness About Orthorexic Behaviors: Coping skills used or Prevention methods
	👍 : ✋ :

ORTHOREXIA
Daily Symptoms Checklist

	SEVERITY	MON	TUES	WED	THUR	FRI	SAT	SUN
WORRYING ABOUT FOOD QUALITY	0-10 Y/N							
AVOID DINING OUT OR CONSUMING FOOD THAT HAS BEEN PREPARED BY OTHERS.	0-10 Y/N							
I'M AFRAID OF BECOMING ILL.	0-10 Y/N							
MANIFEST BODILY INDICATIONS OF MALNUTRITION	0-10 Y/N							
INVEST YOUR TIME ON FOOD RESEARCH.	0-10 Y/N							
REFUSING TO CONSUME A WIDE VARIETY OF MEALS	0-10 Y/N							
YOU'RE AFRAID OF LOSING CONTROL.	0-10 Y/N							
DON'T BE TOO HARSH ON YOUR FRIENDS' EATING CHOICES.	Y/N 0-10							
YOU'RE AFRAID OF LOSING CONTROL.	0-10 Y/N							

ORTHOREXIA DBT RECOVERY WORKSHEET

Date: / /

Sleep quality:

IDENTIFY STRESS-INDUCING BEHAVIORS (ORTHOREXIC BEHAVIORS) AND BELIEFS, THEN REPLACE THEM WITH MORE FLEXIBLE THOUGHTS AND ACTIONS.

✓ ___ : ___

_____
_____
_____

✓ ___ : ___

_____
_____
_____
_____

✓ ___ : ___

_____
_____
_____
_____

A DAILY WIN

_____
_____
_____

Daily Mood Checker

- ANGRY ☐
- ANNOYED ☐
- ANXIOUS ☐
- ASHAMED ☐
- AWKWARD ☐
- BRAVE ☐
- CALM ☐
- CHEERFUL ☐
- CHILL ☐
- CONFUSED ☐
- DISCOURAGED ☐
- DISTRACTED ☐
- EMBARRASSED ☐
- EXCITED ☐
- FRIENDLY ☐
- GUILTY ☐
- HAPPY ☐
- HOPEFUL ☐
- LONELY ☐
- LOVED ☐
- NERVOUS ☐
- OFFENDED ☐
- SCARED ☐
- THOUGHTFUL ☐
- TIRED ☐
- UNCOMFORTABLE ☐
- UNSURE ☐

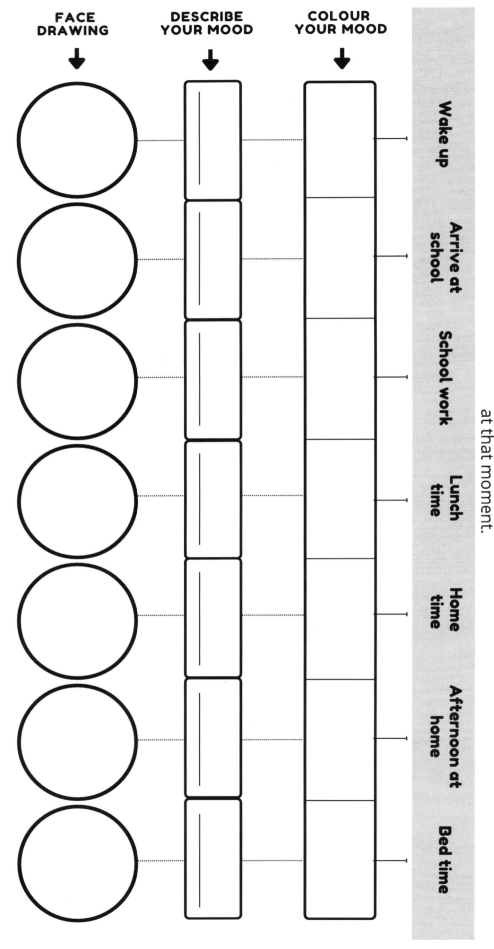

OVERCOMING ORTHOREXIA EPISODES

> In this schedule, try to remain conscious of the nature of this disorder
> Discuss its effect on your feelings and actions, what coping skills do you think work when used at the right time, and how well have you applied these skills?

Orthorexic Behaviors	Awareness About Orthorexic Behaviors: Coping skills used or Prevention methods
	👍 : ✋ :

DATE :   /   /

RATE YOUR PSYCHOLOGICAL SATISFACTION : .... **/10**

WEEKLY EXPOSURE THERAPY WORKSHEET TO GET RIDE OF ORTHOREXIA

This worksheet is useful for eliminating orthorexic behaviors for those with Orthorexia

Description	Rating
Exposure therapy depends on confronting the causes of the problem with courage. So, try to go to a restaurant that serves healthy foods. Take an unhealthy food with you, such as burger slices with pizza, and put it with the food served to you. You will have specific obsessions. Try to overcome these obsessions and eat all your food. *The goal of this procedure is to break the obsession by being bravely exposed to it, and by doing so you will get used to it.*	**TASK** ☐ OBSESSION ○○○○○
Organize or take part in a tour with your friends towards a respectable restaurant. Try to confront your fears about the food served to you. Try to enjoy your time with them at the same time. Do not think about the quality of the food too much, because fear leads to anxiety. *This exercise will stimulate your subconscious mind to eliminate the fear of poor quality food, and maintain your social relationships*	**TASK** ☐ ANXIETY / FEAR OF FOOD ○○○○○
Go to a nearby mountain. Try to camp or sit in it for hours. There, do activities you like, such as reading a book, meditation exercises, yoga, a specific sport. *Take a variety of food.* .... *Reducing anxiety is a major goal of getting rid of this disorder and this procedure will help you build a balance in your feelings*	**TASK** ☐ ENJOYMENT ○○○○○

ONE WAY TO MAKE TOMORROW BETTER:

....

....

ORTHOREXIA
DBT RECOVERY WORKSHEET

Date: / /

Sleep quality:

IDENTIFY STRESS-INDUCING BEHAVIORS (ORTHOREXIC BEHAVIORS) AND BELIEFS, THEN REPLACE THEM WITH MORE FLEXIBLE THOUGHTS AND ACTIONS.

Daily Mood Checker

- [ ] ANGRY
- [ ] ANNOYED
- [ ] ANXIOUS
- [ ] ASHAMED
- [ ] AWKWARD
- [ ] BRAVE
- [ ] CALM
- [ ] CHEERFUL
- [ ] CHILL
- [ ] CONFUSED
- [ ] DISCOURAGED
- [ ] DISTRACTED
- [ ] EMBARRASSED
- [ ] EXCITED
- [ ] FRIENDLY
- [ ] GUILTY
- [ ] HAPPY
- [ ] HOPEFUL
- [ ] LONELY
- [ ] LOVED
- [ ] NERVOUS
- [ ] OFFENDED
- [ ] SCARED
- [ ] THOUGHTFUL
- [ ] TIRED
- [ ] UNCOMFORTABLE
- [ ] UNSURE

A DAILY WIN

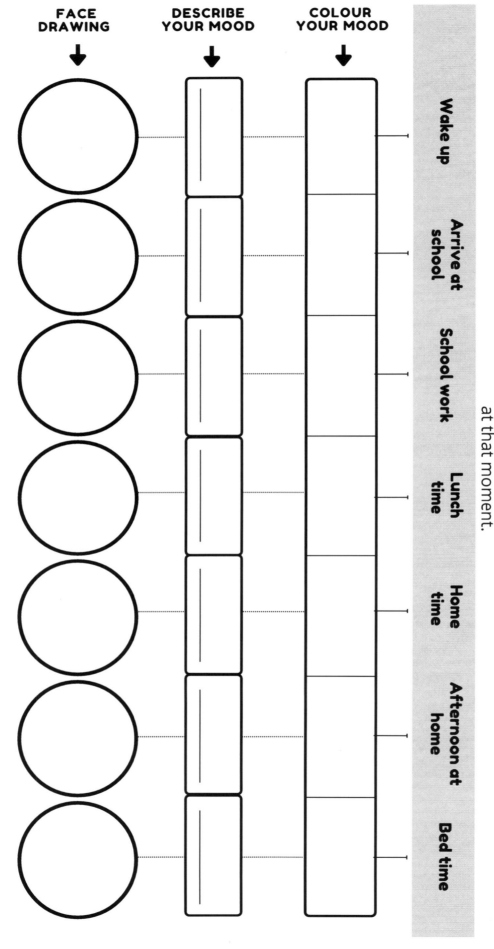

OVERCOMING ORTHOREXIA EPISODES

In this schedule, try to remain conscious of the nature of this disorder
Discuss its effect on your feelings and actions, what coping skills do you think work when used at the right time, and how well have you applied these skills?

Orthorexic Behaviors	Awareness About Orthorexic Behaviors: Coping skills used or Prevention methods
	👍 : ✋ :

ORTHOREXIA
Daily Symptoms Checklist

	SEVERITY	MON	TUES	WED	THUR	FRI	SAT	SUN
WORRYING ABOUT FOOD QUALITY	0-10 Y/N							
AVOID DINING OUT OR CONSUMING FOOD THAT HAS BEEN PREPARED BY OTHERS.	0-10 Y/N							
I'M AFRAID OF BECOMING ILL.	0-10 Y/N							
MANIFEST BODILY INDICATIONS OF MALNUTRITION	0-10 Y/N							
INVEST YOUR TIME ON FOOD RESEARCH.	0-10 Y/N							
REFUSING TO CONSUME A WIDE VARIETY OF MEALS	0-10 Y/N							
YOU'RE AFRAID OF LOSING CONTROL.	0-10 Y/N							
DON'T BE TOO HARSH ON YOUR FRIENDS' EATING CHOICES.	Y/N 0-10							
YOU'RE AFRAID OF LOSING CONTROL.	0-10 Y/N							

ORTHOREXIA
DBT RECOVERY WORKSHEET

Date: / /

Sleep quality:

IDENTIFY STRESS-INDUCING BEHAVIORS (ORTHOREXIC BEHAVIORS) AND BELIEFS, THEN REPLACE THEM WITH MORE FLEXIBLE THOUGHTS AND ACTIONS.

Daily Mood Checker

✓ ___ : ___

✓ ___ : ___

✓ ___ : ___

- ANGRY ☐
- ANNOYED ☐
- ANXIOUS ☐
- ASHAMED ☐
- AWKWARD ☐
- BRAVE ☐
- CALM ☐
- CHEERFUL ☐
- CHILL ☐
- CONFUSED ☐
- DISCOURAGED ☐
- DISTRACTED ☐
- EMBARRASSED ☐
- EXCITED ☐
- FRIENDLY ☐
- GUILTY ☐
- HAPPY ☐
- HOPEFUL ☐
- LONELY ☐
- LOVED ☐
- NERVOUS ☐
- OFFENDED ☐
- SCARED ☐
- THOUGHTFUL ☐
- TIRED ☐
- UNCOMFORTABLE ☐
- UNSURE ☐

A DAILY WIN

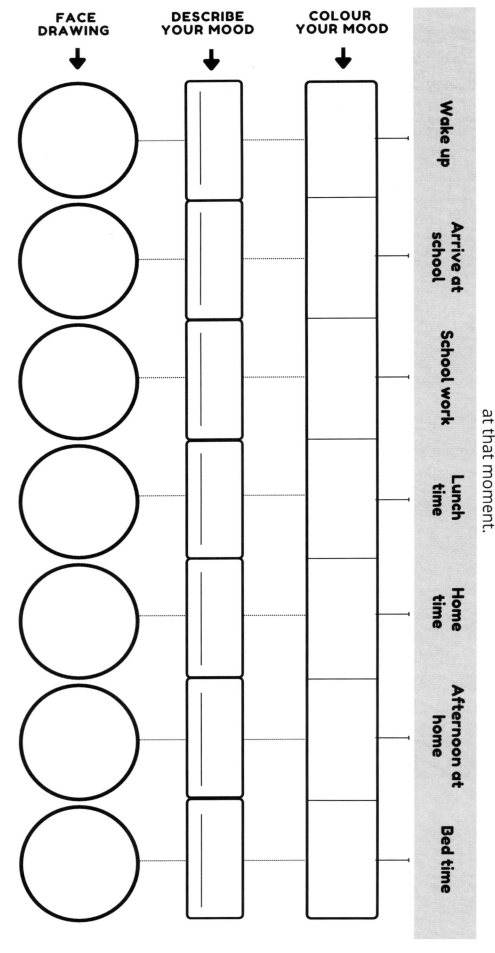

OVERCOMING ORTHOREXIA EPISODES

> In this schedule, try to remain conscious of the nature of this disorder
> Discuss its effect on your feelings and actions, what coping skills do you think work when used at the right time, and how well have you applied these skills?

Orthorexic Behaviors	Awareness About Orthorexic Behaviors: Coping skills used or Prevention methods
	👍 : ✋ :

DATE :   /   /

RATE YOUR PSYCHOLOGICAL SATISFACTION : .... /10

WEEKLY EXPOSURE THERAPY WORKSHEET TO GET RIDE OF ORTHOREXIA

This worksheet is useful for eliminating orthorexic behaviors for those with Orthorexia

Exposure therapy depends on confronting the causes of the problem with courage. So, try to go to a restaurant that serves healthy foods. Take an unhealthy food with you, such as burger slices with pizza, and put it with the food served to you. You will have specific obsessions. Try to overcome these obsessions and eat all your food. *The goal of this procedure is to break the obsession by being bravely exposed to it, and by doing so you will get used to it.*	**TASK** ☐ OBSESSION ○ ○ ○ ○ ○
Organize or take part in a tour with your friends towards a respectable restaurant. Try to confront your fears about the food served to you. Try to enjoy your time with them at the same time. Do not think about the quality of the food too much, because fear leads to anxiety. ***This exercise will stimulate your subconscious mind to eliminate the fear of poor quality food, and maintain your social relationships***	**TASK** ☐ ANXIETY / FEAR OF FOOD ○ ○ ○ ○ ○
Go to a nearby mountain. Try to camp or sit in it for hours. There, do activities you like, such as reading a book, meditation exercises, yoga, a specific sport. *Take a variety of food.* .... *Reducing anxiety is a major goal of getting rid of this disorder and this procedure will help you build a balance in your feelings*	**TASK** ☐ ENJOYMENT ○ ○ ○ ○ ○

ONE WAY TO MAKE TOMORROW BETTER:

....

....

ORTHOREXIA
DBT RECOVERY WORKSHEET

IDENTIFY STRESS-INDUCING BEHAVIORS (ORTHOREXIC BEHAVIORS) AND BELIEFS, THEN REPLACE THEM WITH MORE FLEXIBLE THOUGHTS AND ACTIONS.

✓ ___ : ___

_____
_____
_____

✓ ___ : ___

_____
_____
_____

✓ ___ : ___

_____
_____
_____

A DAILY WIN

_____
_____
_____

Date: / /

Sleep quality:

Daily Mood Checker ✓

- ANGRY ☐
- ANNOYED ☐
- ANXIOUS ☐
- ASHAMED ☐
- AWKWARD ☐
- BRAVE ☐
- CALM ☐
- CHEERFUL ☐
- CHILL ☐
- CONFUSED ☐
- DISCOURAGED ☐
- DISTRACTED ☐
- EMBARRASSED ☐
- EXCITED ☐
- FRIENDLY ☐
- GUILTY ☐
- HAPPY ☐
- HOPEFUL ☐
- LONELY ☐
- LOVED ☐
- NERVOUS ☐
- OFFENDED ☐
- SCARED ☐
- THOUGHTFUL ☐
- TIRED ☐
- UNCOMFORTABLE ☐
- UNSURE ☐

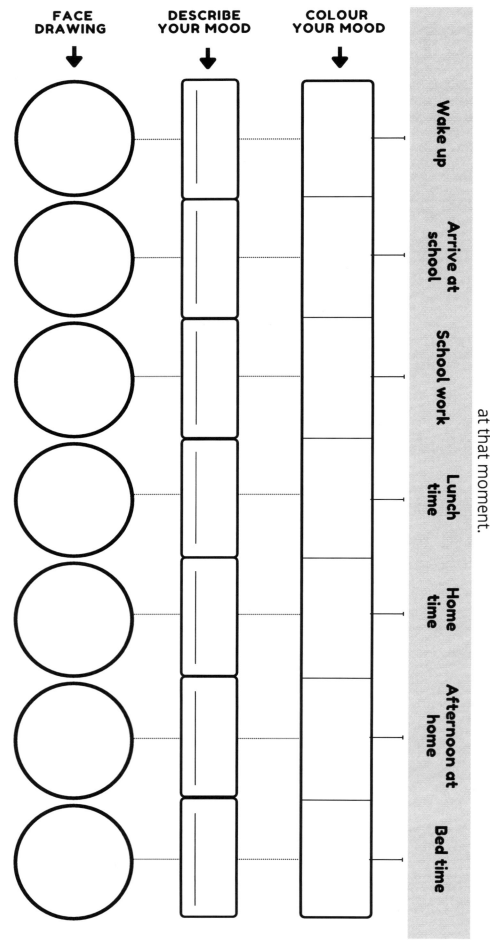

OVERCOMING ORTHOREXIA EPISODES

> In this schedule, try to remain conscious of the nature of this disorder
> Discuss its effect on your feelings and actions, what coping skills do you think work when used at the right time, and how well have you applied these skills?

Orthorexic Behaviors	Awareness About Orthorexic Behaviors: Coping skills used or Prevention methods
	👍 : ✋ :

ORTHORAXIA
Daily Symptoms Checklist

	SEVERITY	MON	TUES	WED	THUR	FRI	SAT	SUN
WORRYING ABOUT FOOD QUALITY	0-10 Y/N							
AVOID DINING OUT OR CONSUMING FOOD THAT HAS BEEN PREPARED BY OTHERS.	0-10 Y/N							
I'M AFRAID OF BECOMING ILL.	0-10 Y/N							
MANIFEST BODILY INDICATIONS OF MALNUTRITION	0-10 Y/N							
INVEST YOUR TIME ON FOOD RESEARCH.	0-10 Y/N							
REFUSING TO CONSUME A WIDE VARIETY OF MEALS	0-10 Y/N							
YOU'RE AFRAID OF LOSING CONTROL.	0-10 Y/N							
DON'T BE TOO HARSH ON YOUR FRIENDS' EATING CHOICES.	Y/N 0-10							
YOU'RE AFRAID OF LOSING CONTROL.	0-10 Y/N							

ORTHOREXIA
DBT RECOVERY WORKSHEET

Date: / /

Sleep quality:

IDENTIFY STRESS-INDUCING BEHAVIORS (ORTHOREXIC BEHAVIORS) AND BELIEFS, THEN REPLACE THEM WITH MORE FLEXIBLE THOUGHTS AND ACTIONS.

Daily Mood Checker ✓

- ANGRY ☐
- ANNOYED ☐
- ANXIOUS ☐
- ASHAMED ☐
- AWKWARD ☐
- BRAVE ☐
- CALM ☐
- CHEERFUL ☐
- CHILL ☐
- CONFUSED ☐
- DISCOURAGED ☐
- DISTRACTED ☐
- EMBARRASSED ☐
- EXCITED ☐
- FRIENDLY ☐
- GUILTY ☐
- HAPPY ☐
- HOPEFUL ☐
- LONELY ☐
- LOVED ☐
- NERVOUS ☐
- OFFENDED ☐
- SCARED ☐
- THOUGHTFUL ☐
- TIRED ☐
- UNCOMFORTABLE ☐
- UNSURE ☐

✓ __:__

_____
_____
_____

✓ __:__

_____
_____
_____

✓ __:__

_____
_____
_____

A DAILY WIN

_____
_____
_____

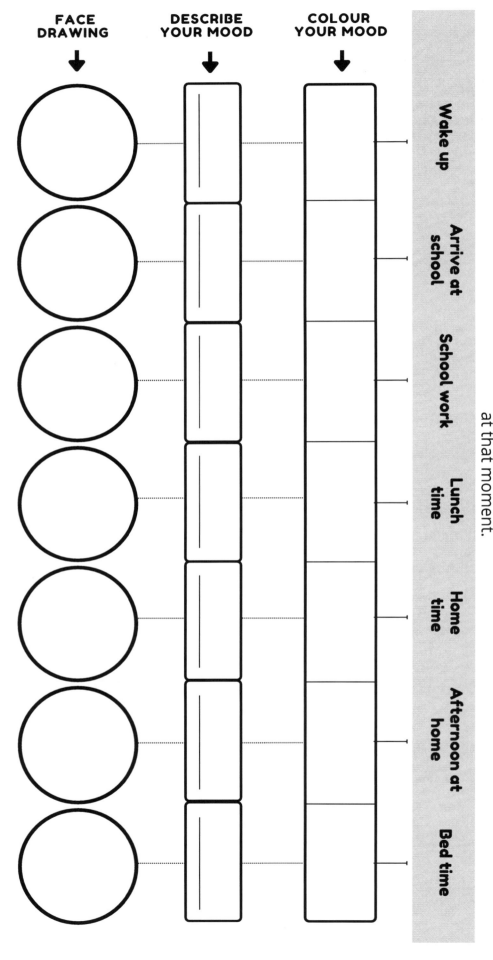

OVERCOMING ORTHOREXIA EPISODES

In this schedule, try to remain conscious of the nature of this disorder
Discuss its effect on your feelings and actions, what coping skills do you think work when used at the right time, and how well have you applied these skills?

Orthorexic Behaviors	Awareness About Orthorexic Behaviors: Coping skills used or Prevention methods
	👍 : ✋ :

DATE : / /

RATE YOUR PSYCHOLOGICAL SATISFACTION : .... /10

WEEKLY EXPOSURE THERAPY WORKSHEET TO GET RIDE OF ORTHOREXIA

This worksheet is useful for eliminating orthorexic behaviors for those with Orthorexia

Description	Rating
Exposure therapy depends on confronting the causes of the problem with courage. So, try to go to a restaurant that serves healthy foods. Take an unhealthy food with you, such as burger slices with pizza, and put it with the food served to you. You will have specific obsessions. Try to overcome these obsessions and eat all your food. *The goal of this procedure is to break the obsession by being bravely exposed to it, and by doing so you will get used to it.*	**TASK** ☐ OBSESSION ○○○○○
Organize or take part in a tour with your friends towards a respectable restaurant. Try to confront your fears about the food served to you. Try to enjoy your time with them at the same time. Do not think about the quality of the food too much, because fear leads to anxiety. *This exercise will stimulate your subconscious mind to eliminate the fear of poor quality food, and maintain your social relationships*	**TASK** ☐ ANXIETY / FEAR OF FOOD ○○○○○
Go to a nearby mountain. Try to camp or sit in it for hours. There, do activities you like, such as reading a book, meditation exercises, yoga, a specific sport. Take a variety of food. .... *Reducing anxiety is a major goal of getting rid of this disorder and this procedure will help you build a balance in your feelings*	**TASK** ☐ ENJOYMENT ○○○○○

ONE WAY TO MAKE TOMORROW BETTER:

....

....

ORTHOREXIA
DBT RECOVERY WORKSHEET

Date: / /

Sleep quality:

IDENTIFY STRESS-INDUCING BEHAVIORS (ORTHOREXIC BEHAVIORS) AND BELIEFS, THEN REPLACE THEM WITH MORE FLEXIBLE THOUGHTS AND ACTIONS.

Daily Mood Checker

- [ ] ANGRY
- [ ] ANNOYED
- [ ] ANXIOUS
- [ ] ASHAMED
- [ ] AWKWARD
- [ ] BRAVE
- [ ] CALM
- [ ] CHEERFUL
- [ ] CHILL
- [ ] CONFUSED
- [ ] DISCOURAGED
- [ ] DISTRACTED
- [ ] EMBARRASSED
- [ ] EXCITED
- [ ] FRIENDLY
- [ ] GUILTY
- [ ] HAPPY
- [ ] HOPEFUL
- [ ] LONELY
- [ ] LOVED
- [ ] NERVOUS
- [ ] OFFENDED
- [ ] SCARED
- [ ] THOUGHTFUL
- [ ] TIRED
- [ ] UNCOMFORTABLE
- [ ] UNSURE

✓ ___:___

_____
_____
_____

✓ ___:___

_____
_____
_____
_____

✓ ___:___

_____
_____
_____
_____

A DAILY WIN

_____
_____
_____

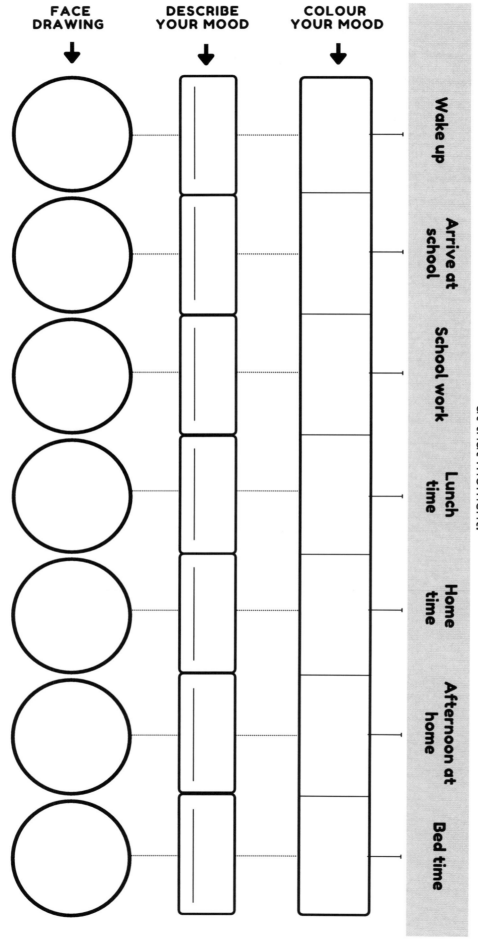

OVERCOMING ORTHOREXIA EPISODES

In this schedule, try to remain conscious of the nature of this disorder
Discuss its effect on your feelings and actions, what coping skills do you think work when used at the right time, and how well have you applied these skills?

Orthorexic Behaviors	Awareness About Orthorexic Behaviors: Coping skills used or Prevention methods
	👍 : ✋ :

ORTHOREXIA
Daily Symptoms Checklist

	SEVERITY	MON	TUES	WED	THUR	FRI	SAT	SUN
WORRYING ABOUT FOOD QUALITY	0-10 Y/N							
AVOID DINING OUT OR CONSUMING FOOD THAT HAS BEEN PREPARED BY OTHERS.	0-10 Y/N							
I'M AFRAID OF BECOMING ILL.	0-10 Y/N							
MANIFEST BODILY INDICATIONS OF MALNUTRITION	0-10 Y/N							
INVEST YOUR TIME ON FOOD RESEARCH.	0-10 Y/N							
REFUSING TO CONSUME A WIDE VARIETY OF MEALS	0-10 Y/N							
YOU'RE AFRAID OF LOSING CONTROL.	0-10 Y/N							
DON'T BE TOO HARSH ON YOUR FRIENDS' EATING CHOICES.	Y/N 0-10							
YOU'RE AFRAID OF LOSING CONTROL.	0-10 Y/N							

ORTHOREXIA
DBT RECOVERY WORKSHEET

Date: / /

Sleep quality:

IDENTIFY STRESS-INDUCING BEHAVIORS (ORTHOREXIC BEHAVIORS) AND BELIEFS, THEN REPLACE THEM WITH MORE FLEXIBLE THOUGHTS AND ACTIONS.

Daily Mood Checker

☑ ___ : ___

_____
_____
_____

☑ ___ : ___

_____
_____
_____

☑ ___ : ___

_____
_____
_____
_____

A DAILY WIN

_____
_____
_____

- ANGRY ☐
- ANNOYED ☐
- ANXIOUS ☐
- ASHAMED ☐
- AWKWARD ☐
- BRAVE ☐
- CALM ☐
- CHEERFUL ☐
- CHILL ☐
- CONFUSED ☐
- DISCOURAGED ☐
- DISTRACTED ☐
- EMBARRASSED ☐
- EXCITED ☐
- FRIENDLY ☐
- GUILTY ☐
- HAPPY ☐
- HOPEFUL ☐
- LONELY ☐
- LOVED ☐
- NERVOUS ☐
- OFFENDED ☐
- SCARED ☐
- THOUGHTFUL ☐
- TIRED ☐
- UNCOMFORTABLE ☐
- UNSURE ☐

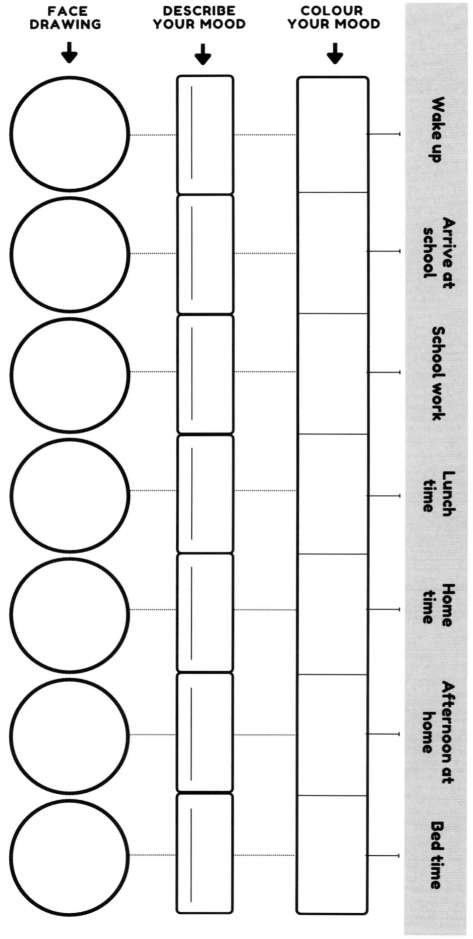

OVERCOMING ORTHOREXIA EPISODES

> In this schedule, try to remain conscious of the nature of this disorder
> Discuss its effect on your feelings and actions, what coping skills do you think work when used at the right time, and how well have you applied these skills?

Orthorexic Behaviors	Awareness About Orthorexic Behaviors: Coping skills used or Prevention methods
	👍 : ✋ :

DATE :   /   /

RATE YOUR PSYCHOLOGICAL SATISFACTION : .... /10

WEEKLY EXPOSURE THERAPY WORKSHEET TO GET RIDE OF ORTHOREXIA

This worksheet is useful for eliminating orthorexic behaviors for those with Orthorexia

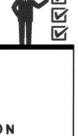

Exposure therapy depends on confronting the causes of the problem with courage. So, try to go to a restaurant that serves healthy foods. Take an unhealthy food with you, such as burger slices with pizza, and put it with the food served to you. You will have specific obsessions. Try to overcome these obsessions and eat all your food. *The goal of this procedure is to break the obsession by being bravely exposed to it, and by doing so you will get used to it.*	**TASK** ☐ OBSESSION ○○○○○
Organize or take part in a tour with your friends towards a respectable restaurant. Try to confront your fears about the food served to you. Try to enjoy your time with them at the same time. Do not think about the quality of the food too much, because fear leads to anxiety. *This exercise will stimulate your subconscious mind to eliminate the fear of poor quality food, and maintain your social relationships*	**TASK** ☐ ANXIETY / FEAR OF FOOD ○○○○○
Go to a nearby mountain. Try to camp or sit in it for hours. There, do activities you like, such as reading a book, meditation exercises, yoga, a specific sport. *Take a variety of food.* .... *Reducing anxiety is a major goal of getting rid of this disorder and this procedure will help you build a balance in your feelings*	**TASK** ☐ ENJOYMENT ○○○○○

ONE WAY TO MAKE TOMORROW BETTER:

....

....

ORTHOREXIA
DBT RECOVERY WORKSHEET

Date: / /

Sleep quality:

IDENTIFY STRESS-INDUCING BEHAVIORS (ORTHOREXIC BEHAVIORS) AND BELIEFS, THEN REPLACE THEM WITH MORE FLEXIBLE THOUGHTS AND ACTIONS.

✓ ___ : ___

_____
_____
_____

✓ ___ : ___

_____
_____
_____

✓ ___ : ___

_____
_____
_____

A DAILY WIN

_____
_____
_____

Daily Mood Checker

- ANGRY ☐
- ANNOYED ☐
- ANXIOUS ☐
- ASHAMED ☐
- AWKWARD ☐
- BRAVE ☐
- CALM ☐
- CHEERFUL ☐
- CHILL ☐
- CONFUSED ☐
- DISCOURAGED ☐
- DISTRACTED ☐
- EMBARRASSED ☐
- EXCITED ☐
- FRIENDLY ☐
- GUILTY ☐
- HAPPY ☐
- HOPEFUL ☐
- LONELY ☐
- LOVED ☐
- NERVOUS ☐
- OFFENDED ☐
- SCARED ☐
- THOUGHTFUL ☐
- TIRED ☐
- UNCOMFORTABLE ☐
- UNSURE ☐

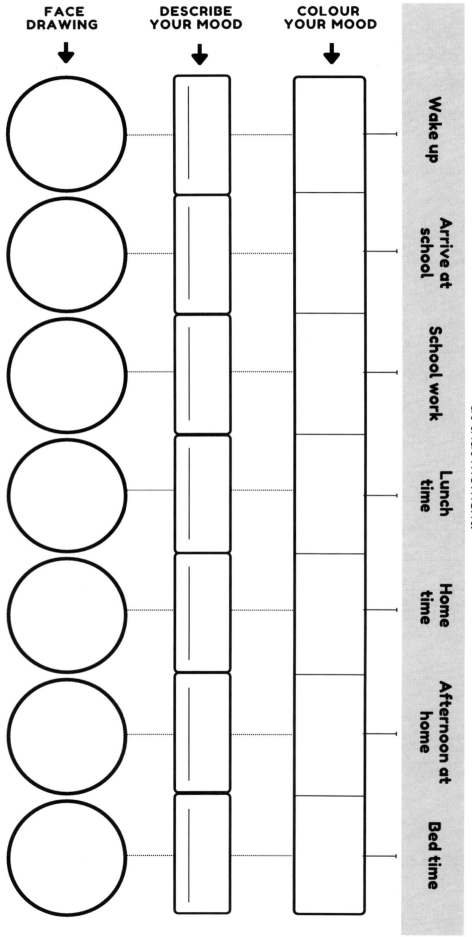

OVERCOMING ORTHOREXIA EPISODES

In this schedule, try to remain conscious of the nature of this disorder
Discuss its effect on your feelings and actions, what coping skills do you think work when used at the right time, and how well have you applied these skills?

Orthorexic Behaviors	Awareness About Orthorexic Behaviors: Coping skills used or Prevention methods
	👍 : ✋ :

ORTHOREXIA
Daily Symptoms Checklist

	SEVERITY	MON	TUES	WED	THUR	FRI	SAT	SUN
WORRYING ABOUT FOOD QUALITY	0-10 Y/N							
AVOID DINING OUT OR CONSUMING FOOD THAT HAS BEEN PREPARED BY OTHERS.	0-10 Y/N							
I'M AFRAID OF BECOMING ILL.	0-10 Y/N							
MANIFEST BODILY INDICATIONS OF MALNUTRITION	0-10 Y/N							
INVEST YOUR TIME ON FOOD RESEARCH.	0-10 Y/N							
REFUSING TO CONSUME A WIDE VARIETY OF MEALS	0-10 Y/N							
YOU'RE AFRAID OF LOSING CONTROL.	0-10 Y/N							
DON'T BE TOO HARSH ON YOUR FRIENDS' EATING CHOICES.	Y/N 0-10							
YOU'RE AFRAID OF LOSING CONTROL.	0-10 Y/N							

ORTHOREXIA
DBT RECOVERY WORKSHEET

Date: / /

Sleep quality:

IDENTIFY STRESS-INDUCING BEHAVIORS (ORTHOREXIC BEHAVIORS) AND BELIEFS, THEN REPLACE THEM WITH MORE FLEXIBLE THOUGHTS AND ACTIONS.

✓ ___ : ___

_____
_____
_____

✓ ___ : ___

_____
_____
_____

✓ ___ : ___

_____
_____
_____

A DAILY WIN

_____
_____
_____

Daily Mood Checker

- ANGRY ☐
- ANNOYED ☐
- ANXIOUS ☐
- ASHAMED ☐
- AWKWARD ☐
- BRAVE ☐
- CALM ☐
- CHEERFUL ☐
- CHILL ☐
- CONFUSED ☐
- DISCOURAGED ☐
- DISTRACTED ☐
- EMBARRASSED ☐
- EXCITED ☐
- FRIENDLY ☐
- GUILTY ☐
- HAPPY ☐
- HOPEFUL ☐
- LONELY ☐
- LOVED ☐
- NERVOUS ☐
- OFFENDED ☐
- SCARED ☐
- THOUGHTFUL ☐
- TIRED ☐
- UNCOMFORTABLE ☐
- UNSURE ☐

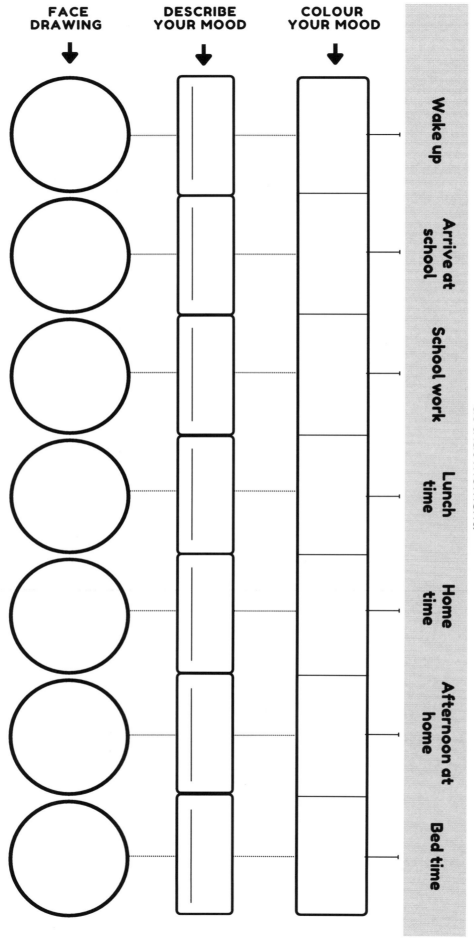

OVERCOMING ORTHOREXIA EPISODES

> In this schedule, try to remain conscious of the nature of this disorder
> Discuss its effect on your feelings and actions, what coping skills do you think work when used at the right time, and how well have you applied these skills?

Orthorexic Behaviors	Awareness About Orthorexic Behaviors: Coping skills used or Prevention methods
	👍 :
	✋ :

DATE : .... / .... / ....

RATE YOUR PSYCHOLOGICAL SATISFACTION : .... /10

WEEKLY EXPOSURE THERAPY WORKSHEET TO GET RIDE OF ORTHOREXIA

This worksheet is useful for eliminating orthorexic behaviors for those with Orthorexia

Exposure therapy depends on confronting the causes of the problem with courage. So, try to go to a restaurant that serves healthy foods. Take an unhealthy food with you, such as burger slices with pizza, and put it with the food served to you. You will have specific obsessions. Try to overcome these obsessions and eat all your food. *The goal of this procedure is to break the obsession by being bravely exposed to it, and by doing so you will get used to it.*	**TASK** ☐ OBSESSION ○○○○○
Organize or take part in a tour with your friends towards a respectable restaurant. Try to confront your fears about the food served to you. Try to enjoy your time with them at the same time. Do not think about the quality of the food too much, because fear leads to anxiety. *This exercise will stimulate your subconscious mind to eliminate the fear of poor quality food, and maintain your social relationships*	**TASK** ☐ ANXIETY / FEAR OF FOOD ○○○○○
Go to a nearby mountain. Try to camp or sit in it for hours. There, do activities you like, such as reading a book, meditation exercises, yoga, a specific sport. *Take a variety of food.* .... *Reducing anxiety is a major goal of getting rid of this disorder and this procedure will help you build a balance in your feelings*	**TASK** ☐ ENJOYMENT ○○○○○

ONE WAY TO MAKE TOMORROW BETTER:

....

....

ORTHOREXIA
DBT RECOVERY WORKSHEET

Date: / /

Sleep quality:

IDENTIFY STRESS-INDUCING BEHAVIORS (ORTHOREXIC BEHAVIORS) AND BELIEFS, THEN REPLACE THEM WITH MORE FLEXIBLE THOUGHTS AND ACTIONS.

✓ ___ : ___

_____
_____
_____

✓ ___ : ___

_____
_____
_____

✓ ___ : ___

_____
_____
_____
_____

Daily Mood Checker ✓

- ANGRY ☐
- ANNOYED ☐
- ANXIOUS ☐
- ASHAMED ☐
- AWKWARD ☐
- BRAVE ☐
- CALM ☐
- CHEERFUL ☐
- CHILL ☐
- CONFUSED ☐
- DISCOURAGED ☐
- DISTRACTED ☐
- EMBARRASSED ☐
- EXCITED ☐
- FRIENDLY ☐
- GUILTY ☐
- HAPPY ☐
- HOPEFUL ☐
- LONELY ☐
- LOVED ☐
- NERVOUS ☐
- OFFENDED ☐
- SCARED ☐
- THOUGHTFUL ☐
- TIRED ☐
- UNCOMFORTABLE ☐
- UNSURE ☐

A DAILY WIN

_____
_____
_____

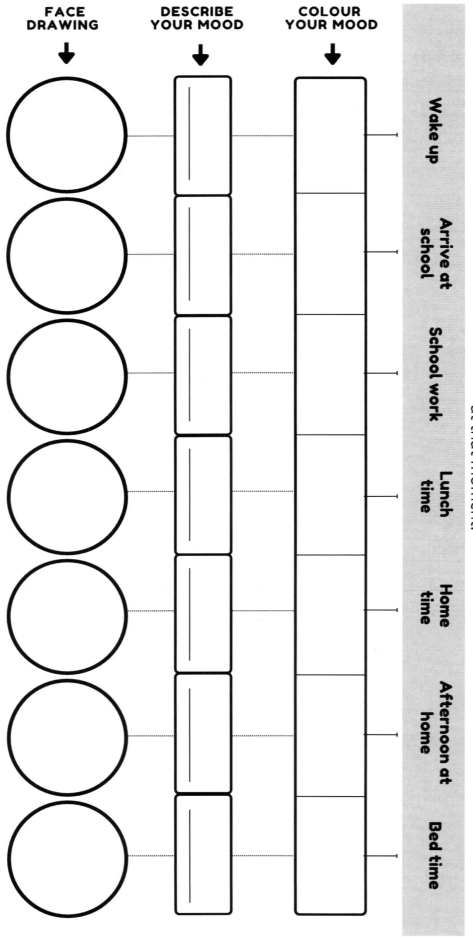

OVERCOMING ORTHOREXIA EPISODES

In this schedule, try to remain conscious of the nature of this disorder
Discuss its effect on your feelings and actions, what coping skills do you think work when used at the right time, and how well have you applied these skills?

Orthorexic Behaviors	Awareness About Orthorexic Behaviors: Coping skills used or Prevention methods
	👍 :
	✋ :

ORTHOREXIA
Daily Symptoms Checklist

	SEVERITY	MON	TUES	WED	THUR	FRI	SAT	SUN
WORRYING ABOUT FOOD QUALITY	0-10 Y/N							
AVOID DINING OUT OR CONSUMING FOOD THAT HAS BEEN PREPARED BY OTHERS.	0-10 Y/N							
I'M AFRAID OF BECOMING ILL.	0-10 Y/N							
MANIFEST BODILY INDICATIONS OF MALNUTRITION	0-10 Y/N							
INVEST YOUR TIME ON FOOD RESEARCH.	0-10 Y/N							
REFUSING TO CONSUME A WIDE VARIETY OF MEALS	0-10 Y/N							
YOU'RE AFRAID OF LOSING CONTROL.	0-10 Y/N							
DON'T BE TOO HARSH ON YOUR FRIENDS' EATING CHOICES.	Y/N 0-10							
YOU'RE AFRAID OF LOSING CONTROL.	0-10 Y/N							

ORTHOREXIA
DBT RECOVERY WORKSHEET

Date: / /

Sleep quality:

IDENTIFY STRESS-INDUCING BEHAVIORS (ORTHOREXIC BEHAVIORS) AND BELIEFS, THEN REPLACE THEM WITH MORE FLEXIBLE THOUGHTS AND ACTIONS.

✓ ___ : ___

_____
_____
_____

✓ ___ : ___

_____
_____
_____
_____

✓ ___ : ___

_____
_____
_____
_____

A DAILY WIN

_____
_____
_____

Daily Mood Checker

- ANGRY ☐
- ANNOYED ☐
- ANXIOUS ☐
- ASHAMED ☐
- AWKWARD ☐
- BRAVE ☐
- CALM ☐
- CHEERFUL ☐
- CHILL ☐
- CONFUSED ☐
- DISCOURAGED ☐
- DISTRACTED ☐
- EMBARRASSED ☐
- EXCITED ☐
- FRIENDLY ☐
- GUILTY ☐
- HAPPY ☐
- HOPEFUL ☐
- LONELY ☐
- LOVED ☐
- NERVOUS ☐
- OFFENDED ☐
- SCARED ☐
- THOUGHTFUL ☐
- TIRED ☐
- UNCOMFORTABLE ☐
- UNSURE ☐

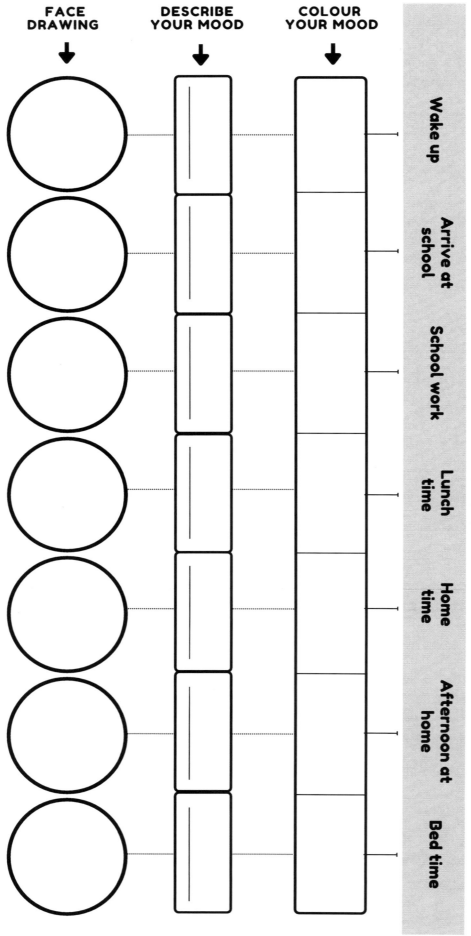

OVERCOMING ORTHOREXIA EPISODES

In this schedule, try to remain conscious of the nature of this disorder
Discuss its effect on your feelings and actions, what coping skills do you think work when used at the right time, and how well have you applied these skills?

Orthorexic Behaviors	Awareness About Orthorexic Behaviors: Coping skills used or Prevention methods
	👍 : ✋ :

DATE : / /

RATE YOUR PSYCHOLOGICAL SATISFACTION : .... /10

WEEKLY EXPOSURE THERAPY WORKSHEET TO GET RIDE OF ORTHOREXIA

This worksheet is useful for eliminating orthorexic behaviors for those with Orthorexia

Exposure therapy depends on confronting the causes of the problem with courage. So, try to go to a restaurant that serves healthy foods. Take an unhealthy food with you, such as burger slices with pizza, and put it with the food served to you. You will have specific obsessions. Try to overcome these obsessions and eat all your food. *The goal of this procedure is to break the obsession by being bravely exposed to it, and by doing so you will get used to it.*	**TASK** ☐ OBSESSION ○○○○○
Organize or take part in a tour with your friends towards a respectable restaurant. Try to confront your fears about the food served to you. Try to enjoy your time with them at the same time. Do not think about the quality of the food too much, because fear leads to anxiety. *This exercise will stimulate your subconscious mind to eliminate the fear of poor quality food, and maintain your social relationships*	**TASK** ☐ ANXIETY / FEAR OF FOOD ○○○○○
Go to a nearby mountain. Try to camp or sit in it for hours. There, do activities you like, such as reading a book, meditation exercises, yoga, a specific sport. *Take a variety of food.* .... *Reducing anxiety is a major goal of getting rid of this disorder and this procedure will help you build a balance in your feelings*	**TASK** ☐ ENJOYMENT ○○○○○

ONE WAY TO MAKE TOMORROW BETTER:

....

....

ORTHOREXIA
DBT RECOVERY WORKSHEET

Date: / /

Sleep quality:

IDENTIFY STRESS-INDUCING BEHAVIORS (ORTHOREXIC BEHAVIORS) AND BELIEFS, THEN REPLACE THEM WITH MORE FLEXIBLE THOUGHTS AND ACTIONS.

✓ ___ : ___

_____

_____

_____

✓ ___ : ___

_____

_____

_____

✓ ___ : ___

_____

_____

_____

A DAILY WIN

_____

_____

Daily Mood Checker ✓

- ANGRY ☐
- ANNOYED ☐
- ANXIOUS ☐
- ASHAMED ☐
- AWKWARD ☐
- BRAVE ☐
- CALM ☐
- CHEERFUL ☐
- CHILL ☐
- CONFUSED ☐
- DISCOURAGED ☐
- DISTRACTED ☐
- EMBARRASSED ☐
- EXCITED ☐
- FRIENDLY ☐
- GUILTY ☐
- HAPPY ☐
- HOPEFUL ☐
- LONELY ☐
- LOVED ☐
- NERVOUS ☐
- OFFENDED ☐
- SCARED ☐
- THOUGHTFUL ☐
- TIRED ☐
- UNCOMFORTABLE ☐
- UNSURE ☐

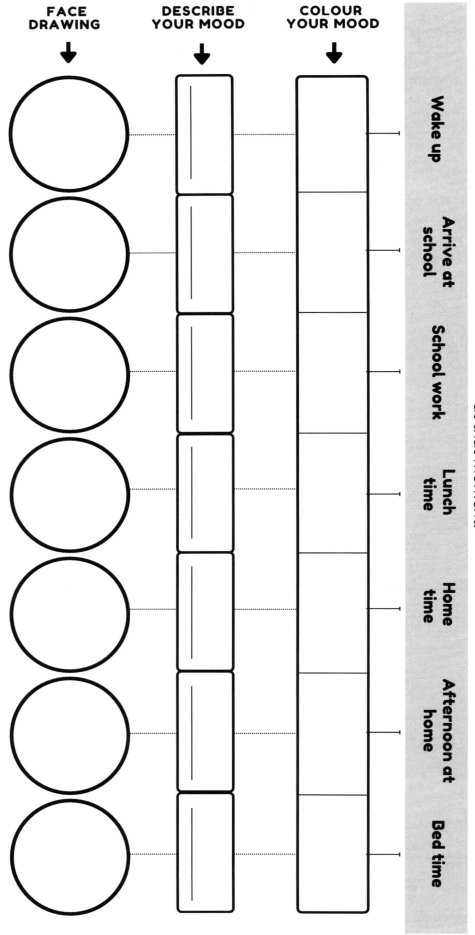

OVERCOMING ORTHOREXIA EPISODES

> In this schedule, try to remain conscious of the nature of this disorder
> Discuss its effect on your feelings and actions, what coping skills do you think work when used at the right time, and how well have you applied these skills?

Orthorexic Behaviors	Awareness About Orthorexic Behaviors: Coping skills used or Prevention methods
	👍 : ✋ :

ORTHOREXIA
Daily Symptoms Checklist

	SEVERITY	MON	TUES	WED	THUR	FRI	SAT	SUN
WORRYING ABOUT FOOD QUALITY	0-10 Y/N							
AVOID DINING OUT OR CONSUMING FOOD THAT HAS BEEN PREPARED BY OTHERS.	0-10 Y/N							
I'M AFRAID OF BECOMING ILL.	0-10 Y/N							
MANIFEST BODILY INDICATIONS OF MALNUTRITION	0-10 Y/N							
INVEST YOUR TIME ON FOOD RESEARCH.	0-10 Y/N							
REFUSING TO CONSUME A WIDE VARIETY OF MEALS	0-10 Y/N							
YOU'RE AFRAID OF LOSING CONTROL.	0-10 Y/N							
DON'T BE TOO HARSH ON YOUR FRIENDS' EATING CHOICES.	Y/N 0-10							
YOU'RE AFRAID OF LOSING CONTROL.	0-10 Y/N							

ORTHOREXIA
DBT RECOVERY WORKSHEET

Date: / /

Sleep quality:

IDENTIFY STRESS-INDUCING BEHAVIORS (ORTHOREXIC BEHAVIORS) AND BELIEFS, THEN REPLACE THEM WITH MORE FLEXIBLE THOUGHTS AND ACTIONS.

Daily Mood Checker ✓

✓ ___ : ___

_____
_____
_____

✓ ___ : ___

_____
_____
_____
_____

✓ ___ : ___

_____
_____
_____
_____

- ANGRY ☐
- ANNOYED ☐
- ANXIOUS ☐
- ASHAMED ☐
- AWKWARD ☐
- BRAVE ☐
- CALM ☐
- CHEERFUL ☐
- CHILL ☐
- CONFUSED ☐
- DISCOURAGED ☐
- DISTRACTED ☐
- EMBARRASSED ☐
- EXCITED ☐
- FRIENDLY ☐
- GUILTY ☐
- HAPPY ☐
- HOPEFUL ☐
- LONELY ☐
- LOVED ☐
- NERVOUS ☐
- OFFENDED ☐
- SCARED ☐
- THOUGHTFUL ☐
- TIRED ☐
- UNCOMFORTABLE ☐
- UNSURE ☐

A DAILY WIN

_____
_____
_____

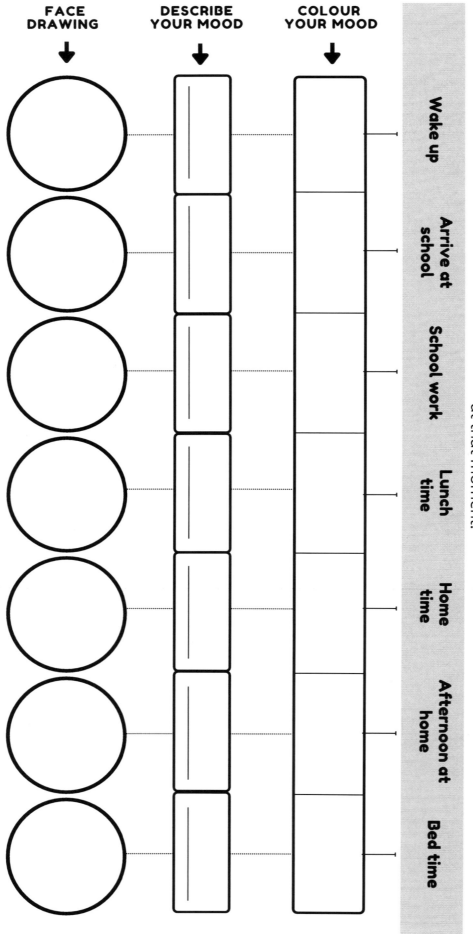

OVERCOMING ORTHOREXIA EPISODES

> In this schedule, try to remain conscious of the nature of this disorder
> Discuss its effect on your feelings and actions, what coping skills do you think work when used at the right time, and how well have you applied these skills?

Orthorexic Behaviors	Awareness About Orthorexic Behaviors: Coping skills used or Prevention methods
	👍 : ✋ :

DATE :   /   /

RATE YOUR PSYCHOLOGICAL SATISFACTION : .... /10

WEEKLY EXPOSURE THERAPY WORKSHEET TO GET RIDE OF ORTHOREXIA

This worksheet is useful for eliminating orthorexic behaviors for those with Orthorexia

Exposure therapy depends on confronting the causes of the problem with courage. So, try to go to a restaurant that serves healthy foods. Take an unhealthy food with you, such as burger slices with pizza, and put it with the food served to you. You will have specific obsessions. Try to overcome these obsessions and eat all your food. *The goal of this procedure is to break the obsession by being bravely exposed to it, and by doing so you will get used to it.*	**TASK** ☐ OBSESSION ○ ○ ○ ○ ○
Organize or take part in a tour with your friends towards a respectable restaurant. Try to confront your fears about the food served to you. Try to enjoy your time with them at the same time. Do not think about the quality of the food too much, because fear leads to anxiety. *This exercise will stimulate your subconscious mind to eliminate the fear of poor quality food, and maintain your social relationships*	**TASK** ☐ ANXIETY / FEAR OF FOOD ○ ○ ○ ○ ○
Go to a nearby mountain. Try to camp or sit in it for hours. There, do activities you like, such as reading a book, meditation exercises, yoga, a specific sport. *Take a variety of food.* .... *Reducing anxiety is a major goal of getting rid of this disorder and this procedure will help you build a balance in your feelings*	**TASK** ☐ ENJOYMENT ○ ○ ○ ○ ○

ONE WAY TO MAKE TOMORROW BETTER:

....

....

ORTHOREXIA
DBT RECOVERY WORKSHEET

Date: / /

Sleep quality:

IDENTIFY STRESS-INDUCING BEHAVIORS (ORTHOREXIC BEHAVIORS) AND BELIEFS, THEN REPLACE THEM WITH MORE FLEXIBLE THOUGHTS AND ACTIONS.

Daily Mood Checker

- [ ] ANGRY
- [ ] ANNOYED
- [ ] ANXIOUS
- [ ] ASHAMED
- [ ] AWKWARD
- [ ] BRAVE
- [ ] CALM
- [ ] CHEERFUL
- [ ] CHILL
- [ ] CONFUSED
- [ ] DISCOURAGED
- [ ] DISTRACTED
- [ ] EMBARRASSED
- [ ] EXCITED
- [ ] FRIENDLY
- [ ] GUILTY
- [ ] HAPPY
- [ ] HOPEFUL
- [ ] LONELY
- [ ] LOVED
- [ ] NERVOUS
- [ ] OFFENDED
- [ ] SCARED
- [ ] THOUGHTFUL
- [ ] TIRED
- [ ] UNCOMFORTABLE
- [ ] UNSURE

⏱ __ : __

_____
_____
_____

⏱ __ : __

_____
_____
_____

⏱ __ : __

_____
_____
_____

A DAILY WIN

_____
_____
_____

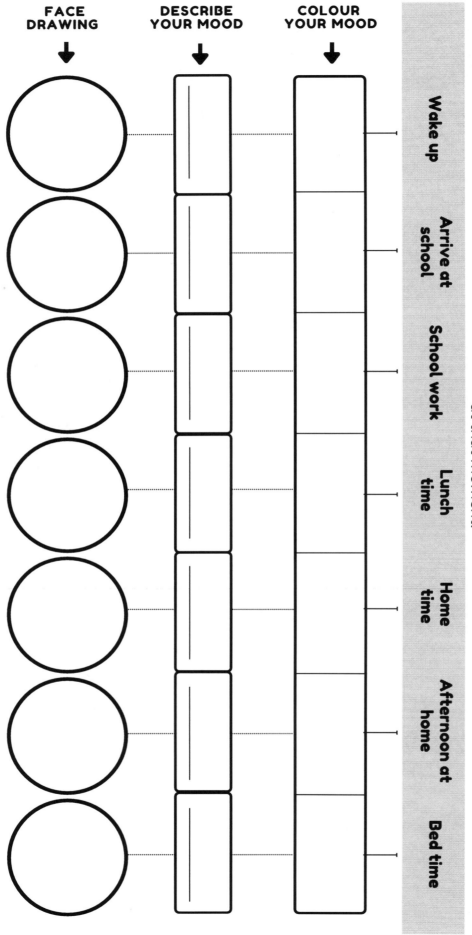

OVERCOMING ORTHOREXIA EPISODES

> In this schedule, try to remain conscious of the nature of this disorder
> Discuss its effect on your feelings and actions, what coping skills do you think work when used at the right time, and how well have you applied these skills?

Orthorexic Behaviors	Awareness About Orthorexic Behaviors: Coping skills used or Prevention methods
	👍 : ✋ :

ORTHOREXIA
Daily Symptoms Checklist

	SEVERITY	MON	TUES	WED	THUR	FRI	SAT	SUN
WORRYING ABOUT FOOD QUALITY	0-10 Y/N							
AVOID DINING OUT OR CONSUMING FOOD THAT HAS BEEN PREPARED BY OTHERS.	0-10 Y/N							
I'M AFRAID OF BECOMING ILL.	0-10 Y/N							
MANIFEST BODILY INDICATIONS OF MALNUTRITION	0-10 Y/N							
INVEST YOUR TIME ON FOOD RESEARCH.	0-10 Y/N							
REFUSING TO CONSUME A WIDE VARIETY OF MEALS	0-10 Y/N							
YOU'RE AFRAID OF LOSING CONTROL.	0-10 Y/N							
DON'T BE TOO HARSH ON YOUR FRIENDS' EATING CHOICES.	Y/N 0-10							
YOU'RE AFRAID OF LOSING CONTROL.	0-10 Y/N							

ORTHOREXIA
DBT RECOVERY WORKSHEET

Date: / /

Sleep quality:

IDENTIFY STRESS-INDUCING BEHAVIORS (ORTHOREXIC BEHAVIORS) AND BELIEFS, THEN REPLACE THEM WITH MORE FLEXIBLE THOUGHTS AND ACTIONS.

Daily Mood Checker

✓ ___ : ___

_____
_____
_____

✓ ___ : ___

_____
_____
_____
_____

✓ ___ : ___

_____
_____
_____
_____
_____

- [ ] ANGRY
- [ ] ANNOYED
- [ ] ANXIOUS
- [ ] ASHAMED
- [ ] AWKWARD
- [ ] BRAVE
- [ ] CALM
- [ ] CHEERFUL
- [ ] CHILL
- [ ] CONFUSED
- [ ] DISCOURAGED
- [ ] DISTRACTED
- [ ] EMBARRASSED
- [ ] EXCITED
- [ ] FRIENDLY
- [ ] GUILTY
- [ ] HAPPY
- [ ] HOPEFUL
- [ ] LONELY
- [ ] LOVED
- [ ] NERVOUS
- [ ] OFFENDED
- [ ] SCARED
- [ ] THOUGHTFUL
- [ ] TIRED
- [ ] UNCOMFORTABLE
- [ ] UNSURE

A DAILY WIN

_____
_____
_____

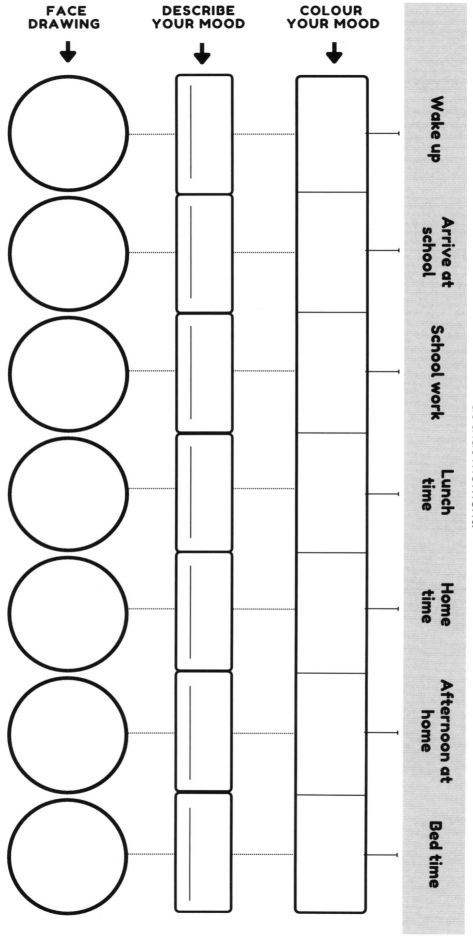

OVERCOMING ORTHOREXIA EPISODES

> In this schedule, try to remain conscious of the nature of this disorder
> Discuss its effect on your feelings and actions, what coping skills do you think work when used at the right time, and how well have you applied these skills?

Orthorexic Behaviors	Awareness About Orthorexic Behaviors: Coping skills used or Prevention methods
	👍 : ✋ :

DATE : / /

RATE YOUR PSYCHOLOGICAL SATISFACTION : .... /10

WEEKLY EXPOSURE THERAPY WORKSHEET TO GET RIDE OF ORTHOREXIA

This worksheet is useful for eliminating orthorexic behaviors for those with Orthorexia

Exposure therapy depends on confronting the causes of the problem with courage. So, try to go to a restaurant that serves healthy foods. Take an unhealthy food with you, such as burger slices with pizza, and put it with the food served to you. You will have specific obsessions. Try to overcome these obsessions and eat all your food. *The goal of this procedure is to break the obsession by being bravely exposed to it, and by doing so you will get used to it.*	**TASK** ☐ OBSESSION ○ ○ ○ ○ ○
Organize or take part in a tour with your friends towards a respectable restaurant. Try to confront your fears about the food served to you. Try to enjoy your time with them at the same time. Do not think about the quality of the food too much, because fear leads to anxiety. *This exercise will stimulate your subconscious mind to eliminate the fear of poor quality food, and maintain your social relationships*	**TASK** ☐ ANXIETY / FEAR OF FOOD ○ ○ ○ ○ ○
Go to a nearby mountain. Try to camp or sit in it for hours. There, do activities you like, such as reading a book, meditation exercises, yoga, a specific sport. *Take a variety of food.* .... *Reducing anxiety is a major goal of getting rid of this disorder and this procedure will help you build a balance in your feelings*	**TASK** ☐ ENJOYMENT ○ ○ ○ ○ ○

ONE WAY TO MAKE TOMORROW BETTER:

....

....

ORTHOREXIA
DBT RECOVERY WORKSHEET

Date: / /

Sleep quality:

IDENTIFY STRESS-INDUCING BEHAVIORS (ORTHOREXIC BEHAVIORS) AND BELIEFS, THEN REPLACE THEM WITH MORE FLEXIBLE THOUGHTS AND ACTIONS.

✓ ___ : ___

_____
_____
_____
_____

✓ ___ : ___

_____
_____
_____
_____

✓ ___ : ___

_____
_____
_____
_____

A DAILY WIN

_____
_____
_____

Daily Mood Checker ✓

- ANGRY ☐
- ANNOYED ☐
- ANXIOUS ☐
- ASHAMED ☐
- AWKWARD ☐
- BRAVE ☐
- CALM ☐
- CHEERFUL ☐
- CHILL ☐
- CONFUSED ☐
- DISCOURAGED ☐
- DISTRACTED ☐
- EMBARRASSED ☐
- EXCITED ☐
- FRIENDLY ☐
- GUILTY ☐
- HAPPY ☐
- HOPEFUL ☐
- LONELY ☐
- LOVED ☐
- NERVOUS ☐
- OFFENDED ☐
- SCARED ☐
- THOUGHTFUL ☐
- TIRED ☐
- UNCOMFORTABLE ☐
- UNSURE ☐

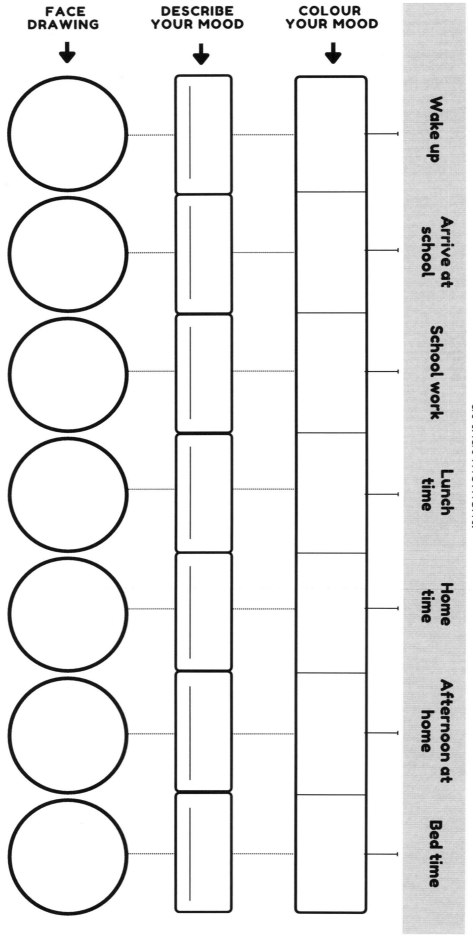

OVERCOMING ORTHOREXIA EPISODES

> In this schedule, try to remain conscious of the nature of this disorder
> Discuss its effect on your feelings and actions, what coping skills do you think work when used at the right time, and how well have you applied these skills?

Orthorexic Behaviors	Awareness About Orthorexic Behaviors: Coping skills used or Prevention methods
	👍 : ✋ :

ORTHOREXIA
Daily Symptoms Checklist

	SEVERITY	MON	TUES	WED	THUR	FRI	SAT	SUN
WORRYING ABOUT FOOD QUALITY	0-10 Y/N							
AVOID DINING OUT OR CONSUMING FOOD THAT HAS BEEN PREPARED BY OTHERS.	0-10 Y/N							
I'M AFRAID OF BECOMING ILL.	0-10 Y/N							
MANIFEST BODILY INDICATIONS OF MALNUTRITION	0-10 Y/N							
INVEST YOUR TIME ON FOOD RESEARCH.	0-10 Y/N							
REFUSING TO CONSUME A WIDE VARIETY OF MEALS	0-10 Y/N							
YOU'RE AFRAID OF LOSING CONTROL.	0-10 Y/N							
DON'T BE TOO HARSH ON YOUR FRIENDS' EATING CHOICES.	Y/N 0-10							
YOU'RE AFRAID OF LOSING CONTROL.	0-10 Y/N							

ORTHOREXIA
DBT RECOVERY WORKSHEET

Date: / /

Sleep quality:

IDENTIFY STRESS-INDUCING BEHAVIORS (ORTHOREXIC BEHAVIORS) AND BELIEFS, THEN REPLACE THEM WITH MORE FLEXIBLE THOUGHTS AND ACTIONS.

Daily Mood Checker

✓ ___:___

_____
_____
_____

✓ ___:___

_____
_____
_____
_____

✓ ___:___

_____
_____
_____
_____

A DAILY WIN

_____
_____
_____

- ANGRY ☐
- ANNOYED ☐
- ANXIOUS ☐
- ASHAMED ☐
- AWKWARD ☐
- BRAVE ☐
- CALM ☐
- CHEERFUL ☐
- CHILL ☐
- CONFUSED ☐
- DISCOURAGED ☐
- DISTRACTED ☐
- EMBARRASSED ☐
- EXCITED ☐
- FRIENDLY ☐
- GUILTY ☐
- HAPPY ☐
- HOPEFUL ☐
- LONELY ☐
- LOVED ☐
- NERVOUS ☐
- OFFENDED ☐
- SCARED ☐
- THOUGHTFUL ☐
- TIRED ☐
- UNCOMFORTABLE ☐
- UNSURE ☐

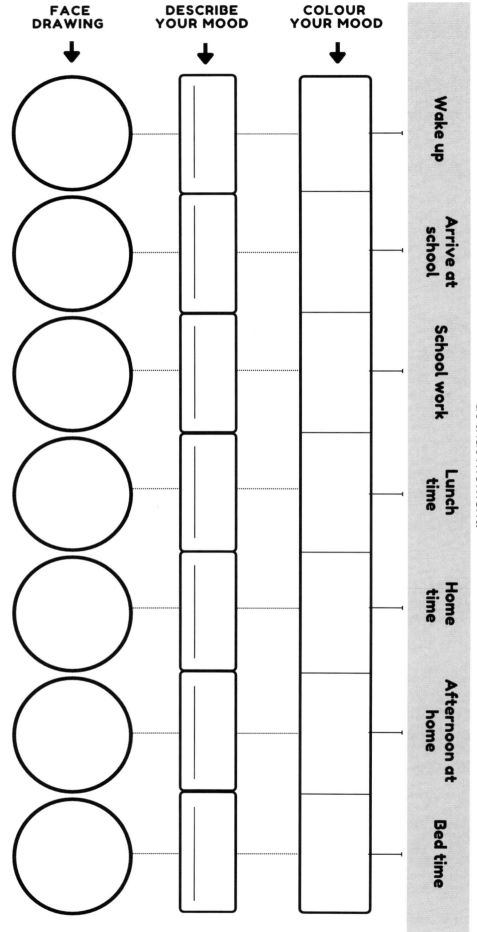

OVERCOMING ORTHOREXIA EPISODES

> In this schedule, try to remain conscious of the nature of this disorder
> Discuss its effect on your feelings and actions, what coping skills do you think work when used at the right time, and how well have you applied these skills?

Orthorexic Behaviors	Awareness About Orthorexic Behaviors: Coping skills used or Prevention methods
	👍 : ✋ :

DATE :   /   /

RATE YOUR PSYCHOLOGICAL SATISFACTION : .... /10

WEEKLY EXPOSURE THERAPY WORKSHEET TO GET RIDE OF ORTHOREXIA

This worksheet is useful for eliminating orthorexic behaviors for those with Orthorexia

Exposure therapy depends on confronting the causes of the problem with courage. So, try to go to a restaurant that serves healthy foods. Take an unhealthy food with you, such as burger slices with pizza, and put it with the food served to you. You will have specific obsessions. Try to overcome these obsessions and eat all your food. *The goal of this procedure is to break the obsession by being bravely exposed to it, and by doing so you will get used to it.*	**TASK** ☐ OBSESSION ○ ○ ○ ○ ○
Organize or take part in a tour with your friends towards a respectable restaurant. Try to confront your fears about the food served to you. Try to enjoy your time with them at the same time. Do not think about the quality of the food too much, because fear leads to anxiety. *This exercise will stimulate your subconscious mind to eliminate the fear of poor quality food, and maintain your social relationships*	**TASK** ☐ ANXIETY / FEAR OF FOOD ○ ○ ○ ○ ○
Go to a nearby mountain. Try to camp or sit in it for hours. There, do activities you like, such as reading a book, meditation exercises, yoga, a specific sport. Take a variety of food. .... *Reducing anxiety is a major goal of getting rid of this disorder and this procedure will help you build a balance in your feelings*	**TASK** ☐ ENJOYMENT ○ ○ ○ ○ ○

ONE WAY TO MAKE TOMORROW BETTER:

....

....

ORTHOREXIA
DBT RECOVERY WORKSHEET

Date: / /

Sleep quality:

IDENTIFY STRESS-INDUCING BEHAVIORS (ORTHOREXIC BEHAVIORS) AND BELIEFS, THEN REPLACE THEM WITH MORE FLEXIBLE THOUGHTS AND ACTIONS.

✓ ___ : ___

_____
_____
_____

✓ ___ : ___

_____
_____
_____
_____

✓ ___ : ___

_____
_____
_____
_____

A DAILY WIN

_____
_____
_____

Daily Mood Checker ✓

- ANGRY ☐
- ANNOYED ☐
- ANXIOUS ☐
- ASHAMED ☐
- AWKWARD ☐
- BRAVE ☐
- CALM ☐
- CHEERFUL ☐
- CHILL ☐
- CONFUSED ☐
- DISCOURAGED ☐
- DISTRACTED ☐
- EMBARRASSED ☐
- EXCITED ☐
- FRIENDLY ☐
- GUILTY ☐
- HAPPY ☐
- HOPEFUL ☐
- LONELY ☐
- LOVED ☐
- NERVOUS ☐
- OFFENDED ☐
- SCARED ☐
- THOUGHTFUL ☐
- TIRED ☐
- UNCOMFORTABLE ☐
- UNSURE ☐

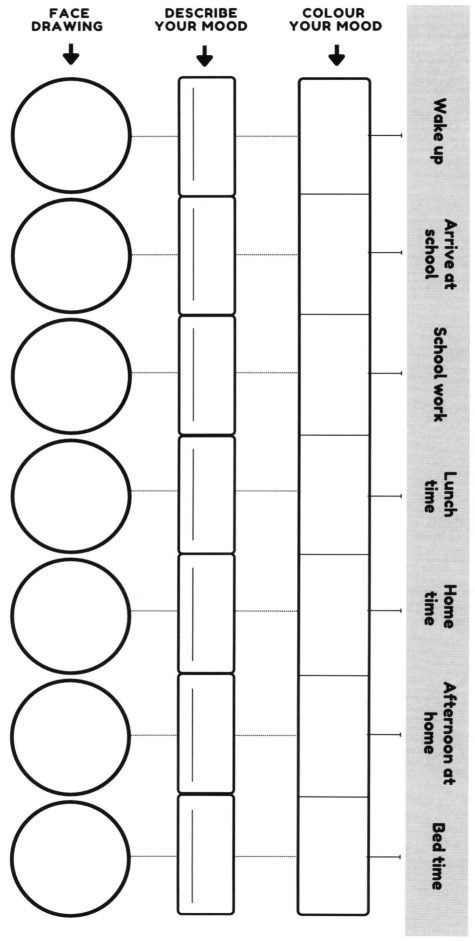

OVERCOMING ORTHOREXIA EPISODES

In this schedule, try to remain conscious of the nature of this disorder
Discuss its effect on your feelings and actions, what coping skills do you think work when used at the right time, and how well have you applied these skills?

Orthorexic Behaviors	Awareness About Orthorexic Behaviors: Coping skills used or Prevention methods
	👍 : ✋ :

Printed in Poland
by Amazon Fulfillment
Poland Sp. z o.o., Wrocław